THE REFERENCE SHELF *(Contiued)*

Volume 23

No.

2. Representative American Speeches: 1950-1951. A. C. Baird. $1.75.

No.

6. Gambling in America. H. L. Marx, Jr. $1.75.

Volume 22

No. 3. Representative American Speeches: 1949-1950. A. C. Baird. $1.75.

Volume 21

No. 2. Representative American Speeches: 1948-1949 A. C. Baird. $1.75.

Volume 20

No.

ederal World Government. J. E. Johnsen. $1.50.

6. Federal Information Controls in Peacetime. R. E. Summers. $1.50.

Volume 19

No. 3. Free Medical Care. C. A. Peters. $1.25.

Volume 18

No.

epresentative American Speeches: 1944-1945. A. C. Baird. $1.25.

. Anatomy of Racial Intolerance. G. B. de Huszar. $1.25.

6. Palestine: Jewish Homeland? J. E. Johnsen. $1.25.

Volume 17

No. 4. Representative American Speeches: 1943-1944. A. C. Baird. $1.25

Volume 16

No.

1. Representative American Speeches: 1941-1942. A. C. Baird. $1.25.

No.

6. Representative American Speeches: 1942-1943. A. C. Baird. $1.25.

THE REFERENCE SHELF

Vol. 28   No. 1

IMMIGRATION
AND THE
UNITED STATES

Edited by
POYNTZ TYLER

THE H. W. WILSON COMPANY
NEW YORK   1956

PREFACE

Immigrants have come to America from many countries and for many reasons. Some sought freedom of worship, some freedom of the mind, some wealth. Many found what they sought, and after finding it seemed reluctant to let others seek it too. They tended to look askance at the latecomer and to feel that his customs, his language, his religion, his very lateness, made him a threat to the peace and prosperity and security of the new land. After three centuries, and in varying degrees, that feeling is still with us, but it is leavened today by a respect for the rights and dignity of man that is inherent in the two points of view—both honest, both sincere—that Americans now hold in regard to immigration.

Some believe that the United States has reached the peak of its growth, culturally and economically, and they seek to preserve what we have. They do not feel that new industries and new ventures will arise to absorb immigration as they have in the past. And they do not believe we can open our doors to all who profess democracy and still remain a refuge of democracy itself.

Others believe we are still growing, still changing, and continually advancing into new frontiers of industry and opportunity. They believe immigration has enriched America's past and will enrich its future, and that a constant but regulated flow of new blood and new brains will guarantee both our strength and our democracy.

These divergent viewpoints, and the divergent solutions to the problem of immigration they naturally engender, are presented in the pages that follow. To the authors of these articles, and to the publishers, the editor extends sincere thanks for permission to reprint.

POYNTZ TYLER

October 25, 1955

CONTENTS

I. HISTORICAL BACKGROUND

EDITOR'S INTRODUCTION

Give me your tired, your poor,
Your huddled masses yearning to breathe free,
The wretched refuse of your teeming shore,
Send these, the homeless, tempest-tossed, to me:
I lift my lamp beside the golden door.
—*Inscription on the Statue of Liberty*

When these lines were written in 1886 by Emma Lazarus, they expressed the feeling of a great many people in the United States. They expressed it for different reasons. To the compassionate they meant what Miss Lazarus meant, that America should be a haven for the poor, the hungry, and the oppressed of all lands. A haven where, freed of the political and social and economic shackles that made them wretched, they could stand upright. Others, millions of others, wanted the lamp to shine bright for more personal reasons. They wanted the golden door held wide because many on those teeming shores, in varying degrees of consanguinity, were their relatives. They wanted to bring families and friends and neighbors to this new land of opportunity and hope. Still others wanted those huddled masses to come here for the sake of America itself. They wanted them, desperately, as hewers of wood and drawers of water.

Whatever prompted their welcome they came—and they came in such numbers that the American Protective Association rose up to bar the gates. This was not our only manifestation of nativism, as the first three articles that follow will show, but it was an inevitable result of an immigration policy that has ever been a strange amalgam of logic and prejudice, altruism and abuse, extravagant hopes and equally extravagant fears. The effects of this hybrid policy on our immediate neighbors and upon our friends throughout the world is dealt with in the remainder of the section—a section that will explain, in some measure, the anomalous position in which immigration has placed us today and in the past.

THE LAMPLIGHTERS [1]

There is a popular mystical theory that the principles of Americanism are derived from our Anglo-Saxon ancestors who lived in the dark forests of Germany. According to this theory, there is something about dark German forests that produces a love of liberty, although the even darker forests of Africa are supposed to have a different effect. A sober view of history compels the reflection that the Anglo-Saxons who inhabited the dark forests of Germany were mostly serfs. . . .

Theories of liberty and democracy had not yet been naturalized in England when the Pilgrims left for Holland and America. Centuries of Plantagenet, Tudor and Stuart despotism had moulded the thinking of Englishmen in 1620. It was decades later that the first defenders of religious liberty and of the freedom of the press, William Penn and John Milton, arose in England, and it was only in the nineteenth century that liberalism and democracy became respectable on British soil.

Even before 1620, however, one nation in Europe was guided by republican principles and the ideal of tolerance. Through the sixteenth and seventeenth centuries, little Holland, welcoming Protestant refugees from Catholic lands, Catholic refugees from Protestant lands, and Jewish refugees from both, had become, with the varied skills those refugees brought, the leader of the world's industry and commerce. So, it was from Holland and not from England that our thirteen colonies first learned the principles of tolerance and democracy. . . .

Liberty is always the child of tolerance. Tolerance develops as a way of life when people realize that strange faces, strange accents and strange ideas do not necessarily portend disaster.

The American way of life is not a product of dark forests nor of any other special sort of scenery, nor yet of any particular blood stream. If political creeds were inherited, our Anglo-Saxon stock would still be royalist. What is distinctive about our ways of living in the United States all emerges from the historic fact

[1] From *Immigration and National Welfare*, pamphlet by Felix S. Cohen, author and lawyer. League for Industrial Democracy. 112 East 19th Street. New York 3. 1940. p29-37. Reprinted by permission.

that our land has been settled by immigrants of many races and many creeds. Out of this diversity of race, tradition, culture and religion grew the need for some political formula that would permit different people to live together in peace. The formulae of human equality, separation of Church and State, universal public education, manhood suffrage and the abolition of ancestral titles, infused with the spirit of tolerance, gave us our American democracy.

The assumption of human equality was necessary and natural in a frontier community where men were on their own and ancestries were irrelevant to the problems of the season. The separation of Church and State was the only formula by which men of many religions could share a common government. Where a society in motion could not know from what group its future leaders would be drawn, the offer of public education had to be made to all children, whatever their race. Where no single racial group constituted a majority of society, political power fell to those groups that were able to join hands across racial chasms and thus to break apart all racial barriers to universal suffrage. Ancestral titles and feudalism never had a chance to develop in a society whose members did not know each other's ancestors.

If you are interested in a man's past life and ancestry, the shibboleth that all men are equal will seem absurd. But if you are interested in the infinite potentialities of human beings and don't know their past lives or ancestors, the formula of human equality is at least a good practical working assumption. And this spirit, which we have called the frontier spirit, was found on the sidewalks of New York as well as in the mining camps of California. The virtues and the vices of men strong enough, good enough, or bad enough to leave families, friends, jobs, and farms in the quest for a new and better life were to be found among those who immigrated to New England from Europe as well as among those who immigrated to Oregon from New England. These virtues and vices of the immigrant endowed the American spirit with its distinctive character. . . .

It is easy to hold to theories of tolerance in years of peace, but the true test of such theories comes in moments of crisis. Such a moment faced the colonists in the summer of 1776 . . .

[when] the combined British and Hessian forces were proving too strong for the gallant resistance of General Washington's little army. On August 14th, 1776, the Continental Congress, having just completed the printing of the Declaration of Independence, and not knowing how long the printed copies could be kept out of the hands of invading troops, turned to consider the problem of the Hessian invaders. The resolution that was adopted was courageous, yet without malice. It bore the stamp of tolerance believed in as a source of strength.

Whereas it has been the wise policy of these states to extend the protection of their laws to all those who should settle among them, of whatever nation or religion they might be, and to admit them to a participation of the benefits of civil and religious freedom; and whereas the benevolence of this practice, as well as its salutary effects, have rendered it worthy of being continued in future times. . .

Resolved, Therefore, that these states will receive all such foreigners who shall leave the arms of his Britannic majesty in America, and shall choose to become members of any of these states; that they shall be protected in the free exercise of their respective religions, and be invested with the rights, privileges and immunities of natives, as established by the laws of these states;

Resolved, That the foregoing resolution be committed to the committee which brought in the report, and that they be directed to have it translated into German.

Thousands of Hessians accepted this invitation and became loyal citizens of Pennsylvania and New Jersey. The promise of land and freedom apparently made a greater impression upon the Hessians than the colonial artillery.

Four score and seven years passed and again the nation's fate rested on the tide of battle. In moments when racial and national hatred is most easily inflamed, the Union found its greatest strength in the welcome it extended to the Negro in the South and to the immigrant from Europe and the Orient. The platform of the Republican Party which Abraham Lincoln helped to write in 1864 declared:

Resolved, That foreign immigration, which in the past has added so much to the wealth, development of resources and increase of power to the nation, the asylum of the oppressed of all nations, shall be fostered and encouraged by a liberal and just policy.

If our country is today the most prosperous nation of the earth, it is, in no small measure—and we are not ignoring the importance of our large natural resources—because our people, richer in tolerance than any other people of the world, have been able to welcome men, women and children of all races, and have been able to live together in peace over an area as large as twenty-five European nations. Living together in peace, the people of each region and each state have contributed to the prosperity rather than to the destruction of every other region and state. Each racial stock and each national group has contributed something of value to our economic life.

If our country is today the most open-minded and the most scientific of the great nations, that, too, is largely a product of our tradition of tolerance. The tremendous advance of the United States in technology has been in a very real sense a consequence of the freedom we have allowed to individual initiative and of our national tolerance towards ideas and enterprises that would have been suppressed as revolutionary, dangerous, or just plumb crazy in a less tolerant society. In our America, millions of human beings have been free to develop along many diverse lines. Many groups and many individuals have been free to make a distinctive contribution to our civilization and our society. . . .

In the long run, the democratic rights of citizens are safe only when the rights of foreigners are protected. History shows that every weapon of persecution prepared and used against those of an alien race has been finally turned to destroy the liberty of all who sanctioned such weapons.

It is no accident that the greatest spokesmen of American democracy have always insisted upon the right of asylum as an essential part of the American dream. The Declaration of Independence, in listing the "repeated injuries and usurpations" of the British sovereign, declared:

> He has endeavored to prevent the population of these States; for that purpose obstructing the Laws for Naturalization of Foreigners; refusing to pass others to encourage their migrations hither, and raising the conditions of new Appropriations of Lands.

In this declaration was echoed the principle enunciated in Section 41 of Magna Charta guaranteeing to all foreign merchants free entry into the country, so long as they are not "of a country at war against us."

It was George Washington who, in his Thanksgiving Day Proclamation of 1795, called upon his fellow citizens, in noting the blessing of peace and freedom which they themselves enjoyed:

. . . humbly and fervently to beseech the kind Author of these blessings . . . to render this country more and more a safe and propitious asylum for the unfortunate of other countries.

This sentiment Thomas Jefferson echoed a few years later:

Shall we refuse to the unhappy fugitives from distress that hospitality which the savages of the wilderness extended to our fathers arriving in this land? Shall oppressed humanity find no asylum on this globe?

Again and again the leaders of our national life and the major political parties have pledged loyalty to these ideals, which our generation has betrayed. And of this betrayal Alfred E. Smith declared:

I have always suspected . . . that some of the more drastic provisions of our laws and some of the national quotas which were established, were fixed on the basis of fantastic Aryan theories rather than American principles.

Civilization is a living thing, born like other living things through a crossing of strains. At each period in the world's history, the crown of civilization has been held by that nation which represented the greatest tolerance of prior cultures.

It was the proud boast of Pericles, when Athens was becoming the commercial and cultural capital of the world: "We throw open our city to the world and never pass decrees to exclude foreigners."

The valleys of the Tigris and Euphrates and of the Nile, the Greek seaports, Rome, Byzantium, Renaissance Italy, Holland, England, all these in the moments of their greatness were cosmopolitan, endeavoring to assimilate what was best in all prior cultures. Hatred of the alien is always the mark of a declining civilization that has lost its capacity to grow and is no longer able to assimilate what is of value in other cultures.

Our American civilization has had, from time to time, its moments of haunting fear and lost nerve. In every generation the prophets of disaster have proclaimed that immigrants with foreign ways would destroy our American way of life. But today we enjoy citizenship in the most powerful and most prosperous nation of the world because these prophets of disaster, in 1797 and since, did not succeed in building a Chinese Wall around our country to exclude "foreign devils" and strange ideas. We have grown greater and more prosperous as a people by reason of each wave of immigration in the past, and those who now seek our shores carry gifts as great as any that earlier pilgrims brought. If we are true to the American spirit of tolerance, we shall profit from those gifts, from the new industries, new consumer demands, new inventions, new contributions to the amenities of life, that these modern pilgrims bear. If America is destined in the decades or centuries ahead to create a culture and a civilization greater than any the earth has yet seen, it will be because each of the races of the earth is free here in America, as nowhere else, to make its highest contribution to the New World of the future.

IMMIGRATION POLICY PRIOR TO WORLD WAR I [2]

More than eighteen million people have entered the port of New York since . . . [the Statue of Liberty] was unveiled. Immigration added a total of thirty-eight million to the American population. The number of immigrants who passed through the gates of New York in a single year in the quarter of a century preceding World War I was greater than all the barbarian forces that brought about the fall of the ancient Roman Empire. New York and other metropolitan centers became a modern Babel of tongues, and the ethnic complexity of many of our American

[2] From an article by Carl Wittke, professor of history and dean of the Graduate School of Western Reserve University, Cleveland, Ohio. *Annals of the American Academy of Political and Social Science*. 262:5-14. March 1949. Reprinted by permission.

cities has become an important feature of our present-day civilization.

Until after the close of the First World War, the gates of this American land of liberty and opportunity stood open and practically unguarded to all who had the courage to risk the great adventure across the Atlantic. Keeping the gates open was a deep-seated American tradition. It was part of the vision of American democracy to welcome men and women of every national origin who wanted to share the peace and prosperity which this country had to offer. Here they might shed the burdens and the strife of the Old World, and join with all men of strong muscles and stout hearts in the building of a new America. It was only when the complicated problems of the new industrialism, and the conflicts in Europe which involved the United States in two world wars, raised issues of hitherto undreamed-of-proportions and complexity, that the United States abandoned its traditional policy of welcoming all comers, and though the gates were left slightly ajar, they were, for all practical purposes, virtually closed after World War I.

Sources of Colonial Population

The blood of 1776 was already a mixed blood. The Anglo-Saxon element predominated overwhelmingly in the colonial population and determined the main features of American political, legal, and social development. But there were sizable German and Scotch-Irish elements in colonial Pennsylvania, and all along the frontier, from the Mohawk in New York to Georgia. The Swedes and the Dutch left the evidences of their language and customs in New York, New Jersey, Pennsylvania, and Delaware; the French Huguenots in New England and in South Carolina; and Spanish and Portuguese Jews in the port towns along the Atlantic seaboard. Many of these early immigrants came as "redemptioners" and indentured servants, who paid for their passage by binding themselves out for years of servitude to masters who bought their contracts from the ship's captain who brought them over. Some were recruited by real estate agents, ship companies, and proprietors like William Penn who had both freedom of conscience and an abundance of land to offer prospective settlers.

In the colonial period there were no restrictions or quota laws, and there was a callous indifference to the immigrant traffic as such. A few feeble attempts were made to ensure a pitifully small minimum of air space for the passengers who were jammed into the dark and crowded holds of immigrant ships, but such regulations proved ineffective and were more generally ignored than enforced.

Even in the colonial period, there were some who feared lest some of these non-English-speaking strangers from Europe might prove unassimilable. An early statute of colonial Pennsylvania was designed to keep out immigrants who might become public charges; oaths of allegiance were required of the newcomers; a small head tax was frequently imposed on the immigrant, and a somewhat higher charge on the ship captain who brought them in; and with the exception of Rhode Island, the colonies had discriminatory legislation against "Papists" and Jews. The first provost of the University of Pennsylvania advocated a vigorous program for the assimilation of non-English immigrants to his Anglo-Saxon, Church of England standards, and he would have denied the suffrage to the "ignorant" for at least twenty years.

The border lawlessness of Scotch-Irish frontiersmen was a constant source of trouble for the Quaker aristocracy who controlled colonial Pennsylvania, and many of the German sects, which had come into the colony by the scores, had strange notions not only about religion but also about secular matters. Their "tender consciences" forbade them to take legal oaths or to render military service, and they insisted on separate religious schools for their children, and helped to delay the public school movement in Pennsylvania until well into the nineteenth century. It is a fact also that many immigrants were dumped upon the colonies by local governments in Europe which no longer wanted to bother with paupers and violators of the law. Great Britain, as well as some of the Continental countries, looked upon America as a dumping ground for undesirables.

The first organized attack on the immigrant in the national period of United States history occurred during the administration of John Adams. It was a time of crisis in Franco-American relations, and an undeclared naval war actually was in progress between the United States and France. Under the pretext of defending the country against French spies and saboteurs, a Federalist Congress enacted the series of laws [the "Alien and Sedition Acts"] which are remembered in history as the "repressive measures" of John Adams' administration. Two alien acts gave the President extraordinary powers to arrest or deport such aliens as he regarded as dangerous to the peace and security of the United States. Though most historians now agree that the laws were unnecessary, they may be defended as measures motivated by genuine considerations for the national security during a period when a violent Gallomania had gripped a considerable portion of the American people. The Naturalization Act, however, with its provision to extend the requirements for citizenship from five to fourteen years, was clearly an attack on the many immigrants and political refugees from Europe who had entered the United States since 1789, largely because of the political upheavals in France and the British Isles during the period of the French Revolution. These newcomers had affiliated with the opposition party led by Jefferson, and as prospective voters, politicians, and officeholders, had joined in the hue and cry against Adams and the Federalists. The loosely drawn Sedition Act virtually made political criticism and opposition a crime.

The debates on these measures indicate that some would have been glad to abolish the naturalization process altogether. Some wanted to deprive the immigrant of all political rights; others were content to keep him from holding public office. The laws were speedily repealed after the Jeffersonians won the election of 1800, and constituted a major reason for the final defeat of the Federalist Party.

The Irish and the Germans

In the period between 1830 and the outbreak of the Civil War, 3.5 million immigrants landed at the port of New York alone, and nearly 1.15 million of that total arrived in the 1840's. Many came from Britain; the Scandinavian tide was slowly beginning to flow toward the American West; and a trickle of immigration was evident from Italy and Austro-Hungary; but the great bulk of this human cargo came from Ireland and Germany.

Ireland was virtually a conquered country, burdened by an alien church, absentee landlords, and crushing economic restrictions imposed by the mother country. For a long time, the people of the "Emerald Isle" had lived on the very edge of famine conditions, and a season of "potato rot" plunged thousands over the brink into starvation and acute suffering. As a result, hordes of Irishmen were ready to expend the last penny of their meager resources to secure passage to America. The voyage to the Promised Land, in horribly overcrowded emigrant ships, proved to be anything but pleasurable, but though there might be "many inconveniences" in the United States, the Irishman was convinced that he would find no "empty bellies."

His resources completely exhausted when he landed at an American port, and without the means to travel inland, the Irishman huddled with his fellow countrymen in the "shantytowns" that sprang into life in the larger American cities of the East, or crowded the hospitals and almshouses as an object of public charity. In the hands of shrewd political bosses, the Irish became willing political tools of the party machines. They were herded to the polls on election day, and fraudulently registered to cast equal votes with the native born. Condemned upon their arrival to the most menial tasks, the Irish performed the lowliest and hardest kind of unskilled physical labor, and with pick and shovel worked in the construction gangs that built our American cities and the canals and railroads that extended into the West.

The Irishman's love of whisky; the rioting and boisterousness that seemed to accompany each payday; the strange dress, uncouth manners, and rough brogue that marked the recent arrivals; the filth and squalor in which many had to live, and their devotion to a church which Americans still viewed as a "foreign church" ruled by a "foreign potentate"—these features convinced many of older stock in the United States that the melting pot was boiling over because of a new ingredient which was likely to prove completely unassimilable.

The majority of the Germans who came before the Civil War came primarily for economic reasons, although among them was a group of political refugees who left their fatherland after the unsuccessful uprisings of 1830 and 1848. These were men of education and social standing, university graduates, pamphleteers, journalists, professional men, and genuine republicans. They gave the rank and file of the German element a political and cultural leadership which no other immigrant group had in the United States at the time. Many Germans went west and took up farming. Others who were highly skilled Old World craftsmen found employment at their old trades, and took part in the beginnings of the American labor and socialist movements. The intellectuals and political refugees stayed in the cities, for the most part, published newspapers, slowly entered the business or profession for which they had been trained, or as refugees who could not find a stable and secure footing again in a new land, sank gradually into oblivion and were forgotten by both their old and their new fatherland.

Although the German element, like the Irish, was in due time recognized as a group that helped mightily in the building of nineteenth-century America, the Germans in the 1850's aroused the suspicions and incurred the enmity of large segments of the older American population. Native Americans referred to the political refugees among them as "hair-lipped, red republicans," wild-eyed reformers and iconoclasts who not only wanted to continue the struggle for the liberation of Europe on American soil, but also attacked venerable American institutions and advocated reform along most radical lines. Many among them were agnostics, freethinkers, and atheists, who had nothing but contempt for American Puritans and "Methodists," and attacked church and clergy in the most intolerant and scurrilous language.

These newcomers regarded slavery as the darkest blot on the escutcheon of a free America, and had no patience with the compromises by which the major parties had managed for decades to postpone the irrepressible conflict. The growing temperance movement struck at the Germans' love for lager beer, and outraged their concept of "personal liberty." Their Continental Sunday was a challenge to American church people, whose notions of Sabbath observance were in sharp conflict with the Germans' Sunday picnics, dances, theater performances, parades, gymnastic exhibitions, and beer gardens.

Finally, it should be added that native workers and small businessmen in every period have resented the competition of foreigners who threatened their standards of labor and wages. In the 1850's the workers were especially alarmed because immigration was breaking down existing rules of apprenticeship, and they demanded a protective tariff for American labor as well as American industry.

Nativism

The point of the preceding discussion is to emphasize that the nativist agitation of the 1840's and 1850's, the most violent in our history, was not directed against allegedly unassimilable groups of "dagos," "wops," and "hunkies" from Slavic or Latin Europe, but against "splay-footed Irish bog trotters" who were importing "Popish idolatries" and Jesuit intrigue, and "dumb" and "damned lop-eared Dutchmen," infidels who lusted for Sunday pleasures, organized "barbarous clubs" to make sure they got them, and consumed indecent quantities of lager beer. Protestant divines alerted their congregations to the incompatibility of the Papacy with American liberty, and pamphlets combining honest arguments for restricting immigration with obscene, pornographic tales about what was supposed to be going on in monasteries and nunneries poured from the printing presses to arouse Americans to a realization of the danger. Mob violence and street fighting were the inevitable consequences of this battle of the books and the pulpits, and the Irish were regularly referred to as dirty, stupid, riotous, intemperate, bigoted, corrupt, and immoral, and the Germans as radicals, infidels, socialists, "red-republicans," desecraters of the Sabbath, and "lager-beer loafers."

In 1844, New York elected a nativist mayor. The 1830's and 1840's were marked by the burning of a convent in New England, bitter fights over parochial schools and Sunday closing laws, and street fighting between Irish Catholics and Protestants.

The 1850's produced "beer riots" in which Germans were involved, and several bloody encounters in Columbus, Cincinnati, New York, Louisville, and elsewhere between native Americans and German organizations, as the latter returned from Sunday outings with bands blaring and spirits stimulated by a day of convivial drinking. Local nativist political parties appeared in the eastern cities, and in 1845 and 1847 native-American conventions demanded twenty-one years' residence for naturalization, the restriction of immigration, and the limitation of officeholding to native Americans.

The whole antiforeign movement of the period before the Civil War reached a climax in the Know-Nothing Party of the 1850's. The natural successor of earlier nativist political groups, the growth of the order was greatly stimulated by the unusually heavy immigration from Ireland and Germany after 1848, and by the corruption and political abuses which marked the elections in many metropolitan centers, and were attributed in large measure to the manipulation of the immigrant vote. Conservative property owners protested that immigation was raising their taxes, and American workmen organized to combat the degradation of their standard of living.

Such considerations, plus a liberal dose of religious bigotry and intolerance, account for the phenomenal rise of the Know-Nothing Party in the 1850's. It was especially strong in Massachusetts, Pennsylvania, and Maryland, and in certain parts of the South. In Massachusetts it elected a governor by a majority of 33,000 and controlled the state legislature, and in at least a half-dozen other states there were governors and legislatures of Know-Nothing persuasion. Horace Greeley believed the Know-Nothings controlled from seventy-five to a hundred seats in Congress, and leading newspapers seriously discussed the likelihood of a Know-Nothing President of the United States by 1856. The movement was not confined to activity at the ballot box. In its train there followed another epidemic of rioting directed against Irish Catholics and German radical organizations, and a new flood of books and pamphlets that reached a new high in intolerance, bigotry, and lurid exaggeration and misrepresentation.

Actually, the movement disappeared about as quickly as it had arisen, and the issues which it had dramatized sank into relative insignificance in view of the rapidly mounting sectional antagonisms over slavery which presently disrupted all existing political party alignments. In their platform and through their representation in state legislatures and the Federal Congress, the Know-Nothings had demanded an end to the admittance of foreign paupers and criminals and to the granting of public lands to unnaturalized residents of the United States; a twenty-one-year residence requirement for American citizenship; the repeal of all state laws which permitted unnaturalized foreigners to vote; Bible reading in the schools; the restriction of office-holding to Americans by "birth, education and training"; and opposition to the power and influence of the Roman Catholic hierarchy.

These issues were vigorously aired in legislative halls, and bills were introduced to translate them into law, but Know-Nothingism accomplished little of practical consequence. During the course of the Civil War the doors to the United States were thrown open wider than ever. The loyal support which naturalized Americans gave to the Union in time of war, and their distinguished record on the battlefields of the Civil War, went far to integrate the adopted citizen with the native born, silenced many of their nativist critics, and opened the doors of political preferment to representatives of foreign-born groups, who could point with pride to their war record and as veterans of the Grand Army of the Republic could claim their share of the spoils of office.

Nativism has been a hardy perennial in the garden of American politics, and the storms of the Civil War and the Reconstruction era did no more than sear its leaves. Some of its roots lived on, underground, ready to sprout again as the flood of "new immigrants" engulfed the United States, particularly in the decades between 1880 and World War I. By that time the older strains had been fairly well assimilated and accepted, and were quite ready to participate in opposition to the newcomers. In contrast with these older, "desirable," and "respectable" immigrants, the mass migrations from eastern and southern Europe represented peoples who spoke strangely alien tongues and came from a political and social background that seemed to raise almost insuperable problems of Americanization.

Nativism came to full bloom again in the American Protective Association movement of the early 1890's and the Ku Klux Klan of the First World War era. Many who had been quite moderate and tolerant in their attitudes now favored a reduction in the total volume of immigration and advocated some kind of test to separate the undesirable from the desirable. Extreme conservatives . . . maintained that the foreigners now entering the United States were coming "to destroy our government . . . and divide our property." The separatist policies of the Catholic Church, whose membership practically doubled in the last quarter of the nineteenth century because of the heavy immigration, and which advocated separate schools and other separate Catholic institutions, played a prominent part in the revival of the nativist agitation. Quarrels over public versus parochial schools and over curricular standards became lively political issues in some communities. Large eastern cities elected Catholic mayors for the first time in their history, and the rapid growth of new and solidly clannish immigrant areas in the urban and industrial centers revived many of the old arguments, and often with good reason, about the manipulation of foreign-born blocs in municipal elections.

The American Protective Association was born in Iowa in 1887, and a half-dozen years later claimed a large membership in some twenty states, especially in the Middle West. Essentially, it represented an anti-Catholic movement; indeed, it admitted foreign-born citizens to membership provided they would agree to have no traffic with Catholics. The bitter opposition of American workers to Slavic, Italian, and other competitors from eastern and southern Europe played its part in building up the APA to its peak strength in 1893 and 1894. The anti-Catholic issue provided the emotional pressure behind the movement, and there was a recurrence of rioting. But the APA also stressed the menace of unrestricted immigration and pointed out the danger to American institutions, now that the "floodgates" were open to the "$9.60 steerage slime" of Europe. It denounced the political manipulation of the "foreign vote," favored increasing the period of residence required for citizenship, and proposed a plan for strictly selective immigration. The APA played a role in some state legislatures, sometimes in close alliance with the Republican party organizations, but it too could not compete successfully for public attention with the larger issues that arose in American politics at the turn of the century.

The Ku Klux Klan, reborn in Georgia in 1915, represents, with its "Nordic cult" and its gospel of "hundred per cent Americanism," the most recent revival of the nativist spirit. It preached "pure Americanism," "white supremacy," "Nordic superiority," and anti-Semitism, and thrived on the "red-baiting" that marked the war period. It was anti-Catholic, anti-Negro, anti-Jew, and antiforeigner generally, though it stressed these issues in varying degrees in various parts of the country. It recruited many typical middle-class Americans who believed that American institutions, and especially the "little red schoolhouse," were seriously threatened by foreigners and Catholics, and that Jews and Negroes needed to be kept in their proper places. The Klan became financially prosperous, and its initial ventures into the arena of politics were surprisingly successful. Eventually, its influence broke down largely because of the racketeering, corruption, and terrorism which marked its fight for the political spoils in several midwestern states.

Federal Legislation Before 1918

The story of Federal legislation dealing with immigration in the period before 1918 can be quickly told. Until well after the Civil War, the individual states had virtually a free hand in setting up whatever local regulations they desired in the field of immigration. Some eastern states imposed mildly restrictive measures on immigrants and the ship companies that brought them in; middle western and western states, on the other hand, eager to encourage settlement in their area, offered attractive concessions to immigrants, and maintained immigration offices and commissioners to direct the stream of Europeans into their respective commonwealths.

Before 1835 there was no Federal legislation on the subject, with the exception of the act of 1819 which for the first time provided for the assembling of statistics on immigration and established a few mild regulations to protect steerage passengers at sea. In 1837 the United States Supreme Court upheld the power of the states to regulate immigration under their police powers. By the middle of the century the Court was ready to assume jurisdiction over aliens who were passengers in foreign commerce, but it continued to uphold the right of the state to impose regulations to protect the public health and morals, provided such regulations did not include the levying of fees or duties on immigrants and were not unreasonable or in conflict with specific Federal enactments. In 1876, however, the Court branded state laws which taxed immigrants and the owners of the vessels on which they came as unconstitutional attempts to regulate foreign commerce, thus virtually forcing the issue upon the attention of Congress. Congressional committees, and Congress as a whole, had several times considered the frauds associated with the naturalization process and had studied proper requirements for citizenship and ways and means to exclude undesirables; but even the bills sponsored during the Know-Nothing period failed of enactment. The law of 1819 was amended in the 1840's to give greater protection to immigrants traveling in steerage, but such amendments were opposed by the nativists, who wanted to make the immigrant traffic less and not more attractive.

During the Civil War, as men were drawn off into the war effort, immigrants were actually recruited abroad, and efforts were made at the ports of arrival to get them to join the Army at once. President Lincoln, in 1864, signed a bill to create the post of Commissioner of Immigration, and to permit the entrance of contract labor from Europe under agreements which legalized as much as twelve months' labor in payment for the immigrant's passage to the United States. Though an immigration office was opened in New York and several contractors took advantage of the new enactment, the law was repealed four years after its passage as a result of strong popular disapproval.

President Grant pointed out the need for Federal legislation on immigration, but the period of national control did not begin until 1882, when, upon recommendation of President Arthur, the first general United States immigration law was enacted. It began the policy of collecting a head tax from all immigrants, and by subsequent legislation the amount was gradually raised from fifty cents to eight dollars. The law also began the practice of exclusion of undesirables, such as lunatics, idiots, convicts, and those likely to become public charges. In 1885 a law was passed to prohibit contract labor, which because of its defects had to be amended two years later. The power to deport those who had gained admission in violation of the laws was first lodged with the Secretary of the Treasury. In 1903 it was transferred to the new Department of Commerce and Labor, and still later, to the Department of Labor.

During the 1880's a series of congressional investigations revealed the inadequacy of existing regulations and the persistence of fraud and evasion. By this time, both major parties were beginning to concern themselves with the desirability of restricting the volume of immigration. In 1891 a new law provided for additional exclusions based on health standards; it included polygamists, as a result of the controversy that had arisen with the Mormons over the admission of Utah. The law forbade the solicitation of labor abroad and created a staff of Federal employees to enforce these restrictions and to provide proper inspection at the ports of entry. Organized labor consistently favored such legislation; Atlantic steamship companies and certain employer groups frequently lobbied against it.

In 1902 the Industrial Commission published an excellent report on the whole subject of immigration. In 1903, following the assassination of President McKinley in 1901 [by Leon Czolgosz, a native-born American anarchist] it was made unlawful to assist in the illegal admission or naturalization of foreign-born anarchists. In 1907 the Immigration Commission was established, and the President was authorized to carry on discussions of the problems of immigration with foreign nations in international conferences. Additional legislation was designed to make illegal and fraudulent entry from the insular possessions into the United

States more difficult, and in 1910 a law was enacted to suppress the traffic in women for immoral purposes.

The problem of Oriental immigration was limited almost exclusively to the Pacific Coast states, where there was violent opposition to Chinese immigrants in the 1860's and 1870's, and later against the Japanese. Various local ordinances and state laws were passed to discriminate against the Oriental in California, and in the case of the Japanese to prohibit the ownership and lease of real estate. Though many of these measures were unconstitutional, they accomplished their immediate purpose. The problems of Chinese immigration were settled rather easily in 1880 by a new treaty in which China surrendered her earlier most-favored-nation status and agreed to the exclusion of her nationals from the United States, with the exception of teachers, students, travelers, and merchants. The year 1882 marked the passage of the first Chinese exclusion act. The problems arising from the immigration of the Japanese to the Pacific Coast proved far more difficult to settle. Japan insisted on equal rights with other nationals, Californians stubbornly clung to their anti-alien land legislation, and the result was a series of misunderstandings between the two countries which played their part in the gradual deterioration of Japanese-American relations in the present century.

In 1897, near the close of President Cleveland's second term, Congress for the first time passed a bill to impose a literacy test on immigrants. Similar bills were passed in the administrations of Taft and Wilson, with the avowed purpose of discriminating against the newer immigrants and in favor of the older groups. The law required demonstration of ability to read and write in English or some other language, but provided generous exemptions for the physically handicapped, for those under sixteen years of age, and for the parents, grandparents, wives, and minor children of admissible immigrants. Presidents Cleveland, Taft, and Wilson all vetoed the legislation and essentially on the same grounds, namely, that a literacy test could only test what opportunities had been open to the immigrant in his native land, and provided no proof of either his intellectual capacity or his moral worth. Finally, in 1917, under the excitement and strains of the

First World War, Congress was able to muster the two-thirds majority necessary to establish the literacy test over the presidential veto.

IMMIGRATION POLICY SINCE WORLD WAR I [3]

In the early years of the present century the open-door policy was subject to serious strains. In the decade 1901-1910 immigration amounted to nearly nine million. . . . In the next few years a rate of a million a year was maintained; after interruption by World War I the tide rose again. Rumors were current that ten million persons, more or less, were waiting in Europe to get visas and transportation to the United States.

The questions naturally arose: Could we absorb such numbers into our economy? Would our social and political unity bear the strain of more "hyphenated" Americans? An accumulation of economic, social, and political factors was brought to bear upon our immigration policy. It seemed to be generally agreed that the rate of immigration needed to be reduced. But the stirring of latent racial and anti-alien prejudices and the growth of isolationist sentiment favored narrowly selective as well as quantitative limitations. Indeed, bills were introduced in Congress for total prohibition of immigration for periods of from one to fifty years.

As a temporary measure, an act of Congress in 1921 put a definite ceiling upon immigration from the Old World. (This meant mainly Europe; few were admitted anyway from Asia or Africa. Limitations on immigration from Canada and Latin America were not considered feasible for various reasons.) A new scheme was devised—the entering wedge of the "national origins" system—limiting the admissible number of any nationality to 3 per cent of the foreign-born members of that nationality residing here according to the 1910 census. In 1924 the base was changed to the 1890 census, the percentage to

[3] From "Give Me Your Tired, Your Poor—", an issue of *Information Service*, a weekly publication of the Central Department of Research and Survey, National Council of the Churches of Christ in the United States of America. *Information Service*. 32:2-3. April 4, 1953. Reprinted by permission.

2 per cent. Thus the total immigration from the Old World was reduced to about 150,000 a year.

The same Act of 1924, however, provided a new formula to be applied on completion of a farther-reaching analysis of the population. It became effective in the fiscal year 1930. Estimates had been made not only of the nationalities of the foreign-born population but also of the national ancestry of the native-born. According to these estimates at least 80 per cent of the 1920 white population was of northern or western European birth or ancestry, 16 per cent of birth or ancestry in southern or eastern Europe, the rest scattering. For the new formula a total of 154,000 was set for all annual quotas, and 150,000 of the total was divided in proportion to the "national-origins" estimates. Unused quotas in any year could not be used in subsequent years or be distributed to other countries. (The Act of 1952 makes no substantial changes.)

The working of the system, during the twenty years 1930-1949 (inclusive), is indicated by the record of quota admissions. Altogether by 1949 less than 25 per cent of the quotas for northern and western Europe had been used, an average of about 30,000 a year. The average for southern and eastern Europe had been near 60 per cent, about 14.5 thousand a year. It should be noted that during certain years of depression (1932-1936) and war (1942-1945) immigration was reduced to a mere trickle, affecting the above averages. (More aliens left in 1931-1936 than were admitted.) Various restrictions in the laws also discouraged or kept out worthy potential immigrants. The theoretical admission of 154,000 quota immigrants a year was obviously a mere fiction in practice.

It should be noted also, however, that substantial numbers of nonquota immigrants from Europe have been admitted under the Act of 1924. The number was about 300 thousand in the twenty years 1930-1949. These were mainly alien wives, husbands, and minor children of American citizens (also some ministers and teachers). . . .

There is no question that the motives underlying the legislation in the 1920's included (1) the isolationist bent of public opinion in the postwar reaction; (2) a widely promoted (and thoroughly disproven) doctrine that because of innate superiority of the Nordic or Aryan race, especially the Anglo-Saxon or Teutonic branch, its dominance in our population must be maintained (even though some immigration of inferior peoples might be tolerable or even necessary to perform certain tasks); (3) a fear among wage-workers that "pauper labor" from abroad would compete with American native labor and keep wages low; (4) a belief that the foreign-born of certain national cultures had a disproportionate inclination toward lawlessness; (5) a fear of introduction of foreign "isms" by promoters of strange cults and social theories and "subversive" agitators threatening the happy status quo of the "American Way"; and (6) a conviction that the flow of immigrants of different languages, customs, and religions—of generally alien cultures—must be limited to numbers readily assimilable, in order to safeguard our national and social unity and order.

Whatever their validity, these motives and arguments based on them appeared frequently in the congressional debates and other discussions of the early 1920's. In thirty years, however, our internal and external relations have undergone great changes. Assertions of superiority of this or that nationality are now confined to smaller groups, and we hear no more of "pauper labor." The problem of adjustability, it appeared, had largely worked itself out. Many of these considerations had now become of little significance. Yet practically the same national-origins quota system was incorporated in the 1952 Act.

In 1947, the Senate authorized investigation and study of the immigration and naturalization system of the United States. This was entrusted to the Judiciary Committee, and carried on by a subcommittee headed by Senator McCarran of Nevada. Nearly three years later their 925-page report was submitted to Congress, and Senator McCarran introduced an "omnibus" bill to codify in one statute all immigration and naturalization laws, with few significant changes. A subcommittee also of the House Judiciary Committee, headed by Representative Walter of Pennsylvania, prepared a substantially similar bill. Early in 1951, new versions of the McCarran and Walter bills, and a bill by Representative Celler of New York, chairman of the House

Judiciary Committee, with some more liberal provisions, were introduced. In joint hearings by the two subcommittees many religious and other organizations expressed vigorous opposition to the McCarran and Walter bills. Senator Humphrey, supported by twelve other senators, then introduced another bill that included many substantive changes, not abolishing the quota system but providing for the annual pooling of unused quotas. But in June 1952, a fourth McCarran bill, with only slight modifications of previous versions, was accepted by both Houses, and then repassed over the President's veto, to become Public Law 414 of the Eighty-second Congress.

INTERNATIONAL IMPLICATIONS OF AMERICAN IMMIGRATION POLICY [4]

Until 1882 the United States had virtually no immigration restrictions. Come one, come all was its policy. The policy was dictated in part by the tremendous natural resources of the United States and the need for labor to assist in their development. Frontier settlement was progressing; new industries were emerging and mass production methods being developed; roads, canals, railroads, and lines of communication established. All this required manpower, trained technicians, adventurous capitalists. Immigration was the answer.

To other countries the policy was beneficial also. The United States served as a safety valve against excessive economic and social pressures at home. Ambitious and restless spirits as well as those who were just plain hungry could relieve their lot by departure for America. Crop failures, religious persecution, overcrowding with low living standards, and political dissatisfaction were among the leading reasons for migration to America. Those who did not go, often found profitable investment opportunities or markets for their goods through friends who did. Thus at the outset a policy of no restrictions was on the whole a good policy for all concerned.

[4] From an article by Paul Wiers, chief of International Trade Statistics, Statistical Office, United Nations. *Annals of the American Academy of Political and Social Science.* 262:39-44. March 1949. Reprinted by permission.

Even during this stage there were those both in the United States and abroad who voiced objections to the flow of migrants. Although their views were not to have a dominant influence on national migration policies until nearly half a century later, they are of interest because they show the deep-rooted nature and persistence of protests against both immigration and emigration.

In the United States objections were founded on various economic, social, and political grounds. The influx of migrants, who were mostly unskilled laborers, was believed even then by some to constitute a danger to the jobs and wage scales of American workers. The tendency of immigrants to settle in cities, especially on the eastern seaboard, was deplored. Objections were made to the congested living conditions of immigrants and their potential danger to the health and accepted morals of the community at large. Evidence was adduced to show the heavy burden of alien pauperism and complaints were frequent that paupers and criminals were assisted by officials of other countries to emigrate to the United States.

In Europe, there were many who did not believe that emigration to the United States was an unmitigated blessing, especially to those left behind. After the Revolutionary War, England viewed emigration to America in a new light. The United States was no longer a colony, but might one day be a rival power. Fears were expressed over the "ruinous drain of the most useful part of the population of the United Kingdom." The view was advanced that emigration costs money and diminishes capital which otherwise might provide employment at home. . . .

Public opinion in Ireland regarding the benefits of migration to America was also divided. It was generally conceded that the emigrant himself would benefit, particularly if he avoided the pitfall of settling on the eastern seaboard and migrated to the interior where opportunities for employment and advancement were greater. On the other hand, some regarded continued emigration as a "diminution of every source of material wealth and a withdrawal of the motive power from the great engine of national prosperity."

The German view toward emigration was similar but, apparently on the part of some writers at least, was colored by a desire that emigrants maintain close ties with the homeland. The growing belief in Germany that if emigration were to benefit the homeland it must be colonial in nature, was commented on by United States Consul Schoenle. Writing from Barmen, Germany, in 1881 he pointed out that the unprecedented exodus was engaging the attention of the Imperial Chancellor, who estimated that in that year alone the army had been deprived of twenty thousand young men. According to Schoenle, private agencies were being established to

organize settlements on a large scale in foreign territories, where Germans should remain dependent, to a certain degree, on the fatherland, and where the national spirit and customs should be upheld and cultivated, and German manufactures be consumed, and thus use the transatlantic brothers in the economical interests of the mother country.

The continuous flow of immigrants is itself proof that, on the whole, immigrants found themselves better off in the United States than in the mother country. Nevertheless, the immigrant was frequently the target of sharp practices by the unscrupulous both before departure and after arrival. Transportation facilities were often deplorable judged even by the standards of the time. Land agents frequently took advantage of immigrants' lack of knowledge of the country; landlords exploited their poverty. While the British Government had special information officers to service immigrants in its colonies, there were none in the United States. This aspect of the migration problem seems to have been largely overlooked during the very early period by both the United States and foreign governments. . . . The provision of information, adequate safeguards, and perhaps financial assistance to migrants is today one of the most promising fields for international action. . . .

The economic character of European emigration began to change in the 1890's. Previously, it had been largely a transfer of farmers from land-hungry countries to a country with free land. Now it became rural to urban migration, a migration which was soon to be joined by people living in rural areas of the United States itself. This was a result of the growing industrialization and urbanization of the United States.

The United States was not alone in this trend toward industrialization. The industrial revolution, which began in Britain, spread to Continental Europe; at first to France and Germany, and later to countries on the periphery such as Italy and Czechoslovakia. The trend toward industrialization and urbanization at home and the realization that much of the immigration to the United States was of an industrial rather than agricultural nature, influenced the attitudes of European governments toward emigration. Besides, with expanding economic opportunities at home, the economic incentives for emigration partially disappeared. Emigration from the northwestern European countries began to decline even before passage of the quota restrictions.

In the United States the passage of the frontier and the competition of laborers for jobs contributed to a changing point of view with regard to the desirability of immigration. Fear that the country would be inundated after World War I led to the adoption of the first quota law, which became operative in 1921. This was followed by the more restrictive . . . quota law of 1924.

Deportation proceedings now became an important part of the work of immigration officials. Difficulties in administering the quota laws resulted in the return of many incoming immigrants from United States ports of entry and in increased hardships, and added to international ill will. To improve the situation, the immigrant was required to secure a visa, and the consular representative to attest to the advisability of his emigration. The return flow of migrants to Europe increased and required the attention of foreign governments. This, combined with the desire of the European countries themselves to promote industrialization, gave rise to national policies directed at discouraging or even prohibiting the outward movement. Fascist Italy, for example, withdrew favors to emigrants such as cheap transportation to ports of embarkation. After July 1928, Italian emigrants had to promise not to have their families follow them abroad. The strongest step was taken by the Soviet Union, which forbade emigration altogether.

THROUGH THE BACK DOOR [5]

A steady stream of aliens pours illegally into the United States over the Canadian line, and the United States Immigration border patrol is so woefully understaffed that it can't begin to catch them all.

The problem is most crucial . . . [in the American village of Rouses Point, New York] on the Canadian border near the north end of Lake Champlain. Chief Patrol Inspector Chester A. Woish has only twenty-six men in forest-green uniform to guard a two-hundred-mile stretch along which more than sixty-five roads cross the border.

He knows that in the year ended June 30 his men apprehended 439 illegal aliens (392 Canadians and 47 Europeans) and also seven operators who were in the business of smuggling aliens across for an average fee of $300 to $500 a head.

But he has no way of knowing or estimating how many aliens were successful in sneaking through his thin green line of watchmen, or how many might have been Communist spies or saboteurs. In his annual report for 1952-1953 Mr. Woish said that the number who got through, without going into guesswork as to who or what they were, could be "considerable."

"What's to stop them?" asks Mr. Woish. "They know our strength, or rather, our weakness. They know that it's very seldom we can have more than one patrol out at a time in a given area. They know we can't give the border twenty-four-hour coverage. The only thing we can do is mix up our tactics and try to keep 'em guessing. But the initiative is always with the smuggler and he always has a very good chance of success."

Ironically, neither the individual alien nor the organized smuggling rings are breaking any Canadian law, and Canada can do nothing about them. Inspector W. A. McFaul, of Canada's Immigration Department, said recently in Montreal that "more than a few" immigrants legally in Canada are crossing every week illegally to the United States.

⁵ From dispatches to the New York *Herald Tribune* by John G. Rogers, correspondent. New York *Herald Tribune*. p3. September 29, 1953. Reprinted by permission.

"This is not a police state," he said. "Once an immigrant is legally in this country, he has freedom of movement."

Actually, Canada is chagrined. . . . She spends millions to encourage immigration [see "Canada's Welcome Mat," Section IV, below]. However, Canadian census figures show that in ten years ending June 1, 1951, 150,000 people were "lost." The assumption is that most of them went south of the border.

Mr. Woish's territory runs from Churubusco, New York, on the west, to Rangeley, Maine, on the east, but the hot spot for illegal entries and smuggling is the New York and Vermont area on each side of Lake Champlain. Most of the cases trace back to Montreal sixty miles to the north, and a number of smuggling rings are known to be operating from there.

One time an Immigration Service agent dressed himself to look like a European immigrant, went up to Montreal and stood outside a church on Sunday morning. In the space of half an hour four different men approached him and whispered would he like to go to the United States.

It is odd that this problem of illegal entry of aliens is troublesome at a time when Canada is experiencing an economic development boom and should offer both to Canadians and Europeans a far greater opportunity than is available in the United States.

Since 1948, when Canada's big immigration program started, some 700,000 immigrants from Europe have come to Canada, and the bulk of them are content there. Mr. Woish believes, however, that about 5 per cent of these, or roughly 35,000, have the United States in mind as ultimate destination.

There are various reasons for this, despite Canada's opportunities. To the foreigner the United States is still the land of gold-paved streets. Relatives already in the United States beckon to the immigrants. Those from warm climates don't like a Canadian winter.

So, Mr. Woish believes, thousands of Europeans who would have to wait years to get on the American quota, take advantage of Canada's immigration invitation and, once arrived there, set about planning how to get into the United States.

Mr. Woish's men have caught the illegal entries in a variety of ways. Some border farmers will cooperate and report suspicious strangers heading south, although others make money by working for the smugglers. Sometimes through sheer luck, the border patrolmen stumble on a car with aliens inside, or come across them on foot at night in an alfalfa field or along a road.

Of the forty-seven Europeans caught last year, there were ten Italians, six Germans, five Greeks, and four each of Yugoslavs, Romanians, Poles and Dutch. Others were Hungarian, Portuguese, Czech, Austrian, Bulgarian, Belgian, Scottish and Danish.

Mr. Woish says that many of the Europeans caught last year spoke English well enough to have melted unnoticed into the American scene. One Pole admitted he had been a Communist party member. One Austrian said he was a cosmic ray physicist looking for a job.

Deportation proceedings were instituted against all, though sometimes a stay is granted as in the case of an Iron Curtain country man who would suffer persecution on return.

THE WETBACKS [6]

In war the dawn of a new day may mean a new attack, or it may bring temporary, uneasy inactivity. But down here on the Mexican border the dawn of each new day, seven days a week, brings the renewal of an unremitting if bloodless battle to stem a never-ending invasion of the United States.

Dawn is when the "wetbacks"—the Mexican border-jumpers who sneak into the United States at a current rate of a million or more a year—daily resume their devious incursions from the south. Since Mexico and the United States have so far been unable to agree on a new migrant labor policy . . . permitting the *legal* importation of Mexican workmen under controlled conditions, the "wetback" problem . . . [continues].

Some of the "wetbacks" move afoot, across scorching desert wastes. Others stow away on freight trains, in box cars, "on

[6] From "Two Every Minute Across the Border," by Gladwin Hill, West Coast correspondent for the New York *Times*. New York *Times Magazine*. p 13. January 31, 1954. Reprinted by permission.

the rods" and even in gondola cars loaded with steel and in empty tank cars—from which, on occasion, they are extracted, dead, in northern yards. Still others, who have rounded up $150 to pay a professional smuggler, travel northward in automobiles and even in San Diego taxis, to Los Angeles, the San Joaquin Valley and the purlieus of San Francisco.

Dawn, stripping from the invading army the cloak of darkness, is when the Border Patrol of the United States Immigration and Naturalization Service daily resumes its unending efforts to catch and deport the "wetbacks."

The contest . . . is so one-sided it is a wonder the Border Patrol has not tossed in the towel long since.

A Mexican bent on entering the United States without legal sanction has 1,600 miles of border to choose from—from Brownsville, Texas, to San Diego, California. For the first 900 miles the line follows the ambling course of the Rio Grande River northward to El Paso, Texas. In some seasons and some places its waters flow deep and treacherously, forcing the invaders to swim for it (thus their name of "wetbacks"). Along much of the Rio Grande and around settlements like El Paso in Texas, Douglas, Nogales and Yuma in Arizona and Calexico in California, the border is fenced and there are gates where customs and immigration formalities are pursued. But anyone can go a short way out of town and go over or around the fence, and the rest of the border is wide open. The Border Patrol has fewer than 1,000 officers to police the 1,600 miles. If the whole force were lined up along the border at once, it still would form no kind of a cordon. In addition, international relations preclude their using weapons or any kind of force unless attacked.

The battle these officers are forced to wage is one of a "defense in depth," extending northward all the way to San Francisco. Surveillance is maintained over the most inviting segments of the border, but most of the work of apprehending illegal aliens is done well "inland"—on foot and horseback, in jeeps and patrol cars, with an array of tactics from road-blocks to aerial reconnaissance. In fact, the patrol, in collaboration with other law enforcement agencies, extends its activities all the way to the Canadian border and the eastern seaboard. The back stairs of Chicago hotels, the steel mills of western Pennsylvania—any place where possible employment may be found is within the sights of the "wetbacks."

But their main concentrations are in southwestern agriculture. Their number is reliably estimated to reach as high as 100,000 at a time in California and the lower Rio Grande Valley of Texas. The total of those caught tells only part of the story, because for every one of these one or more are presumed to go undetected. A majority probably gravitate back to Mexico after a term of work, but others by the thousands try to make their illegal entry permanent.

The typical "wetback" can be described only as a Mexican and a man (occasionally there are women "wetbacks"). He may be an illiterate peasant from Chihuahua, resembling, with his straw hat, serape and sandals, one of Pancho Villa's followers. He may be a relatively sophisticated unemployed industrial worker from Mexico City who has traveled up to a thousand miles to get to the border. He is generally amiable and seldom a tramp. It takes more than ordinary initiative to marshal a grubstake, get to the border and run the Border Patrol's gantlet, all for the purpose of working harder at lower wages than most United States citizens will accept.

Sure, it is technically illegal; the "wetback" may wind up in jail, if caught repeatedly, for as much as two years. But the chances are that, if caught, he will just be dumped back across the border. Every Mexican knows that hundreds of thousands of his compatriots have preceded him on the route and that once he is in the United States an employer can hire him with impunity (under present laws, it must be proved that the employer knowingly harbored an illegal alien, which is difficult). Under these circumstances, the "wetback" feels, Uncle Sam must not mind too much being "invaded."

The Border Patrol's El Centro headquarters is the nerve center of the California sector, which recently has accounted for nearly two-thirds of the 100,000 "wetbacks" rounded up every month. Here Chief Patrol Officer Ed Parker, working under the Immigration Service's district headquarters in Los Angeles, directs a corps of men whose activities range from checking passports at border gates to camping out in the desert along well-worn "wetback" trails.

Every morning the pilot of the sector, Patrolman Fred Voight, takes off in a Cessna from a near-by airport. Armed with a detailed tract map of all the cotton, fruit and vegetable ranches in the area, he cruises up and down the lush Imperial Valley looking for telltale clusters of itinerants and concentrations of field hands around the establishments of those who are known to employ "wetbacks."

Most "wetbacks" have to pause at least briefly in the valley to work and get a little money before pushing northward. One objective of the patrol is to nail them before they can get Social Security cards. (The law does not deny cards even to illegal aliens and, once in hand, they become quasi-passports.)

The cat-and-mouse game would be comic if it were not for its evil ramifications. Because of their numbers, the "wetbacks" make a mockery of border supervision, transforming the line into a gateway through which foreigners of any sort can infiltrate. The "wetbacks" bring all kinds of contraband with them, from drugs and parrots to venereal disease. Their direct social cost in Imperial County alone, counting everything from jailing to hospitalization for tuberculosis, has been reckoned at several hundred thousand dollars a year.) Many find protective concealment among the half-million Spanish-speaking citizens of the Southwest or in the Latin-American colonies of big cities and proceed to stay here indefinitely, contributing to such problems as poverty and illegitimacy.

The underlying cause of the "wetback" influx is the fact that southwestern agriculture, with its vast expanses of cotton, fruit and vegetables in Texas, New Mexico, Arizona and California, has managed to a degree to turn the clock back a full generation with respect to labor. Like some major segments of eastern industry before World War I, the Southwest today relies extensively on cheap labor. It comes from three sources: the impoverished migratory farm workers, the lowest stratum of our citizen labor force, who number in the hundreds of thousands; "temporary" foreign labor, chiefly Mexican, who have been legally imported under intergovernmental agreements at a rate of 200,000 a year; and the "wetbacks."

To one degree or another, all three categories have to work for whatever they can manage to get. The legally imported "braceros," whose status has been under question by the Mexican and United States governments, nominally get the "prevailing wage" in the area where they work; but what is "prevailing" is established primarily on the say-so of the farmers of that area, and hence is seldom any higher than necessary. Seventy-five cents an hour is a typical current rate—before deductions for transportation, lodging, food, etc. Migrants and "wetbacks" have virtually no protection under Federal and state minimum-wage standards. Pay for the "wetbacks," as fugitives from justice, is often as little as 20 cents an hour, and if they are caught and deported before they can collect their wages it is exactly nothing.

This picture was set forth in 1951 by the nonpartisan lay commission appointed by President Truman to study the "wetback" situation and migratory labor problems in general, and it has never been seriously contested.

The farmer, naturally, views the situation differently. When it is time to plant, cultivate or harvest his crops, he needs labor quickly, for short periods. There are seldom enough resident farm workers in the area and often not enough transient citizen workers. Therefore he seeks foreign labor.

Many farmers deplore the influx of "wetbacks" and will not use them, but others have no compunctions. Some say they need "wetback" workers because the legal importation program is too complicated, slow and inadequate. Some claim they have no way of distinguishing between "wetbacks" and citizen Mexican-Americans. Some simply declare that there is, technically, no law against employing "wetback" labor as long as you don't question an applicant too closely about his origins.

The result is a vicious economic circle that has been turning ever since Mexicans were imported on a large scale during the World War II manpower shortage. The availability of migratory and particularly alien labor (in Texas, "wetbacks" have forced thousands of migrants out of the area) demonstrably depresses wage levels, not only on farms but also in urban occupations.

Resident domestic farm labor as a result has steadily gravitated to more lucrative work. And because this labor is no longer available to the farmers they have had increasing recourse to the migrant-bracero-"wetback" supply.

The plaint about the unavailability of domestic labor, President Truman's commission observed, is similar to the arguments advanced by industry a generation ago against imposing barriers to the immigration of cheap labor from Europe. To suggestions that they might try stabilizing their domestic labor supply, the cheap-labor users have two standard answers: they would go broke (although many have a margin of affluence permitting the use of Cadillacs for field chores); and even if they tried it, it wouldn't work.

Some agricultural economists feel that the situation has reached a point where there is a degree of alarming truth in the latter argument: alien competition has undoubtedly stripped some sections of domestic labor. But this is all the more reason, they say, for interrupting the advance before it gets any worse. What has happened in the last decade, they suggest, could be undone in an equal or shorter period of time.

How?

The Truman commission recommended that the Border Patrol be strengthened; that effective penalties be imposed on the employers of "wetbacks"; that wages and working conditions, including Social Security and unemployment insurance, be improved sufficiently to attract domestic labor; and that the importation of alien labor not be increased. Although these recommendations were endorsed by President Truman, they have not been carried out because of opposition from spokesmen in Congress for southwestern farmers.

On a trip here last August [1953] Attorney General Herbert Brownell Jr. called the "wetback" situation "shocking" and vowed, with President Eisenhower's concurrence, to do something about it. This declaration was quickly countered by complaints from farmers that without "wetbacks" they would lose their crops, and by a clamor for the mass legalization of the "wetbacks" aleady here into *braceros*.

There the matter stands. Once again there are bills before Congress to carry out the Truman commission program. Mr. Brownell reputedly has formulated an anti-"wetback" program, to be broached either legislatively or administratively. The effectiveness of any measures, many regional observers feel, will depend on recognition of the fact that the "wetback" is not an isolated curiosity but essentially alien labor in an unfamiliar guise—a bracero who simply sidestepped the formalities of the legal importation which the United States Government itself has been sponsoring.

The passage of two more years of "wetbackism" since the Truman commission report in 1951 has underscored the importance of the questions the report posed: Does the American public want to continue espousing, directly or indirectly, a foreign labor supply for one segment of the nation's agriculture—a sponsorship which contradicts a generation-old economic policy against importing cheap labor? Does it want to continue to spend millions of dollars a year in importation and apprehension activities? Does it want to go on maintaining what amounts to a 1,600-mile gateway for a variety of evils which are being combated successfully on other fronts?

Meanwhile, at the rate of more than 100,000 a month, more than 3,000 a day, more than two every minute, "wetbacks" continue to stream in. And each dawn the battle against them is renewed.

WHY THEY COME [7]

The force that drives Mexicans northward across the border is an old and simple one. It is poverty. Mexico has less than one acre of arable land per capita (the United States has 2.57), and its agricultural practices are primitive and wasteful.

To make matters worse, slight improvements in sanitary conditions and a normally high birthrate have sent Mexico's population soaring in recent years. Six million people have been added in the past ten years. The annual increment is about 3 per cent, twice that in the United States.

[7] From "Hungry Workers, Ripe Crops, and the Nonexistent Mexican Border," by Richard P. Eckels, free lance writer. *Reporter.* 10:28-32. April 13, 1954. Copyright 1954 by The Reporter Magazine Company. Reprinted by permission.

What President Ruiz Cortines calls "Mexico's ancestral poverty" has been further intensified by years of drought. In many localities, even where irrigation facilities exist, the dams are nearly dry. In the state of Durango alone, 40 per cent of the cattle perished last year: 379,200 head, worth $8.7 million locally. Some climatologists believe that the dry cycle will come to an end about 1960; others believe that a large part of Mexico will continue to be dry for the duration of this geological epoch. At any rate, no informed person expects improvements in the near future.

On top of all these troubles, Mexico has experienced a severe inflation recently. Prices rose 25 per cent in the first year of the Korean War. Mexico's economy has become so dependent upon that of the United States that 81 per cent of all Mexico's imports come from the United States and 85 per cent of its exports go to the United States. Mexico's minerals, cotton, and coffee help pay for American-made trucks, tractors, automobiles, petroleum products, drugs, canned goods, and clothing. . . .

So far as the official figures show, the American tourist is the principal source of dollar income to Mexico, roughly $200 million a year. The total amount sent back to Mexico by migrant workers is impossible to determine, but the amounts known to flow through approved channels suggest that the total could be even larger than the tourist revenue. Added, both sums approximate the entire national budget of Mexico. Thus even the export-import figures do not fully represent Mexico's actual dependence on the United States.

Juan Fulano, the average peon, has one foot in each economy. Representing over 60 per cent of Mexico's population, he earns only 20 per cent of its income, and the gap is widening. If he can find work at all, he can earn fifty-five cents to a dollar a day. He grows his own corn and beans, the rains permitting, but everything he buys—shirt, pants, and shoes—carries contemporary Chicago prices. A pair of blue jeans costs him at least three days' work, a pair of field shoes six days' work.

And so the displaced peons, fleeing starvation, seeking work, stream northward out of the eastern Gulf states—Tamaulipas and Veracruz; out of central Mexico—Zacatecas, San Luis Potosí,

Guanajuato, and the Federal District around Mexico City; out of the western seaboard—Sonora, Sinaloa, Nayarit, Jalisco, Michoacán. They come from an area that extends two thousand miles deep into Mexican territory. On a single morning I found men, ranging in age from eighteen to twenty-seven, from all these states working in a few cotton fields near El Centro, California.

The fugitives from poverty do not start out, as many people suppose, from the immediate vicinity of the border. Nor do they conform, ethnologically, to anyone's stereotype of what a Mexican peon looks like. Some, despite names like Manuel García Ramírez, are blue-eyed, fair-skinned, and light-haired, and could pass for Scandinavians. The only evident common denominator is that they all speak Spanish and suffer from advanced malnutrition: On the average, they weigh about a hundred pounds.

Many of the workers I met told me that they had been lured north by reports of a boom in Mexico's newest state, Baja California, and that they had not originally intended to cross the border into the United States at all. In 1920 the population of Baja California was 20,000; today it is 280,000. Most of the increase has been the result of migration from impoverished areas in central Mexico.

Baja California's Mexicali Valley, the Mexican continuation of California's Imperial Valley, gets its water from the Colorado River. It grows cotton, alfalfa, flax, grains, citrus fruits, olives, and cattle. Jai alai, horse and dog racing, curio shops, and bars bring throngs of American tourists across the border for a quick look at Tijuana. The busiest port of entry on either the Canadian or Mexican border is little San Ysidro, fifteen miles south of San Diego.

But there is scant possibility of a Michoacán peon's being readily absorbed in the glittering artificiality of Tijuana, and hardly more in the agricultural economy of the Mexicali Valley. Flourishing as it is, Baja California can absorb only a small fraction of teeming Mexico's surplus millions.

And so the peons cross the border. Mexican laborers and farm hands have been doing it for years. During the First

World War Mexican labor was utilized even in the steel mills of Pennsylvania; during the Second World War some two hundred thousand Mexicans were imported to assist with crops and to work on railroad section gangs.

What had been extremely informal arrangements were formalized under the Ellender Act of 1951. Recruiting centers were set up in inland Mexican cities, manned by teams of officials representing the United States Employment Service. Trainloads of screened men were taken to employment centers north of the border and there distributed according to an orderly plan.

Ranchers guaranteed prevailing wages, provided housing and meals at a uniform cost of $1.75 a day, and posted bonds to assure the repatriation of their temporary workers after periods of six weeks to six months. According to the *California Farmer,* it cost a rancher an average of fifty dollars to put a Mexican contract laborer to work.

Last year [1953], 197,100 Mexican nationals were processed at a cost of $2.65 million. . . . Of the 94,200 harvest workers accepted through July 31, 1953, California got some 32,000. But farm leaders insist that California needs at least 300,000 harvest hands and that Mexico is the only possible source of "stoop labor."

The word readily gets around Mexicali that even though there is only a boomlet there, unlimited numbers of *braceros* can be utilized over in the United States. In this situation, the legal niceties are ignored. . . .

The long, loud public agitation over the migrant laborers has tended to obscure the fact that other and more dangerous visitors may be coming through our leaking borders.

The Border Patrol says that it has found only a few foreign agents among the Mexican immigrants. But the officers concede that they would have a difficult time running down an alien who had enough money to look well nourished and even fairly well groomed, who could provide himself with spurious documents, buy a ticket to a point a few hundred miles inland, and who had friends to shelter him when he arrived there.

No one knows how much livestock is being stolen or smuggled from ranches in northern Mexico and driven across the

Rio Grande. During the past year, leaders of only two cattle-smuggling plots have been convicted. American stockmen are still nervous about foot-and-mouth disease even though the most recent outbreak was some nine hundred miles from the border. With tick-infested cattle and with horses suffering from a venereal disease called dourine roaming across the line, the Bureau of Animal Industry plans to resume its own patrol with airplanes, jeeps, and mounted riders.

Counterfeit bills in twenty- and fifty-dollar denominations that have turned up recently in southern California have been traced to Mexico. A twenty-two-year-old Mexican with a Greek surname carrying $2,650 in counterfeit fifty-dollar bills fell under suspicion chiefly because he was driving a glittering new sedan of an expensive make. Suppose he had been clever enough to hike across the unfenced desert?

Each month about a million dollars' worth of narcotics, including marijuana, is seized at border points. In view of the border's largely imaginary nature, the quantities successfully smuggled could be a dozen or a hundred times as great.

There is no end to the rackets and no limit to the profits when the border leaks so notoriously.

Many ranchers seem to feel that the problem could be solved by doing away with red tape and issuing a simple crossing card to Mexican laborers. "They need the work," the ranchers say, "and we need their labor."

But how many cards would have to be issued—five hundred thousand or five million? How would the quota be coordinated with the ranchers' demands, fluctuating both seasonally and from year to year? Would the ranchers be willing to have the workers checked for tuberculosis, venereal diseases, criminal connections, subversive activities, and so forth? If so, a lot of highly trained specialists would be needed in the processing line, and the processing costs would run up to $10 a head, and we would still have the problem of how to deal with those who chose to make a broken-field run around left end.

The crisis at the border begins with the crisis in Mexico itself. Mexico's population is growing too rapidly for the progress it is making in opening new lands to settlement and cultivation, in extending irrigation and modernizing its agricultural practices. Mexico is further harried by inflation and drought, possibly threatened by long-term dryness.

And yet Mexico is a proud and ambitious nation. The Mexican government has invested $58 million in increasing domestic production of wheat, corn, and beans, the staples of minimum diet. As stop-gap measures, it is importing frijoles from South Africa and selling flour to bakers at about 60 per cent of cost.

The Administration of President Ruiz Cortines is pushing its "march-to-the-sea" program. Now that yellow fever is under control, the sparsely populated territories of southern Baja California and Quintana Roo are being opened to colonization.

Mexico hopes to expand its fishing fleet and seine the adjacent seas for inexpensive proteins. It is developing its harbors and connecting them by improved roads with inland areas, hoping to develop its coastal shipping and foreign trade.

New highways are being constructed to Baja California, to connect the scattered mines, vineyards, citrus and olive groves, breweries and wineries, and the rich 330,000-acre cotton fields around Mexicali. The port city of Ensenada is undergoing a $15-million program of harbor development.

With all these activities—and some more help from the United States—Mexico's future need not be entirely dark.

Some of Mexico's publicists glibly predict that it will one day be able to support a trebled population of eighty million in comfort and prosperity. In that millennial event, one may infer, the farm-factories of the West and Southwest would have to look elsewhere for cheap labor. But that crisis is still far distant.

II. THE MAKINGS OF AMERICA

EDITOR'S INTRODUCTION

The ethnic pattern of America, as Nathan Glazer points out in the opening article of this section, is not only impossible to analyze, it is impossible even to isolate. There is not an ethnologist living who would attempt a serious explanation of the biological makeup of the typical American, for as artists and advertisers have wasted time and money to discover, there is no typical American. Sinclair Lewis gave the classic definition of him in describing Martin Arrowsmith, the hero of one of his novels. "Martin," he said, "was . . . a Typical Pure-bred Anglo-Saxon American, which means he was a union of German, French, Scotch, Irish, perhaps a little Spanish, conceivably a little of the strains lumped together as 'Jewish,' and a great deal of English, which is itself a combination of Primitive Briton, Celt, Phoenician, Roman, German, Dane, and Swede."

Other writers have been less exact. To them we are "a fusion of cultures," "a blending of bloodstreams," "a nation of mongrels." Possibly all are correct, even though none explains the real paradox that is America—a heterogeneous race but a homogeneous nation.

The section that follows will not resolve that paradox, either, but it will give the reader an inkling of how that paradox came to be. And the articles on the influx of Puerto Ricans—strangers from within our own borders—will give him an idea of why that paradox must continue.

"MELTING POT" OR "NATION OF NATIONS"? [1]

The fact that Americans are also—and in many cases, primarily—Germans, Italians, Poles, Jews, etc. is taken with deadly

[1] From "America's Ethnic Pattern" by Nathan Glazer, associate editor of *Commentary* and a frequent contributor to other periodicals. *Commentary*. 15:401-8. April 1953. Reprinted by permission.

seriousness by the general mass of Americans, but tends rather to be ignored by contemporary writers on social problems, and perhaps more ignored by academic writers than by popular ones. There was a time when the problem of creating an English-speaking nation, with a common loyalty, out of a population at least half of which stems from non-English-speaking peoples was a major subject of discussion in this country. It was during the time of that discussion—roughly the first twenty-five years of this century—that two quite contradictory concepts were developed which have since dominated the consideration of this problem. . . .

It would make things simple if the two concepts of the "melting pot" and the "nation of nations" could be assigned to different periods—if we could believe, as so many do, that the earlier American immigrants (Germans, Irish, Norwegians, Swedes, English) did indeed assimilate rapidly, and that for them the "melting pot" worked; while the later immigrants—Italians, Jews, Poles, Slovaks, South Slavs, Greeks, and so on—did not assimilate as rapidly, and that to them the "nation of nations" concept was applicable.

Actually, on the basis of the facts, one could more easily argue the opposite. An important section of the major element in the earlier migration—the Germans—came with just the idea of creating a nation of their countrymen in America. In the 1830's there was considerable agitation among disappointed German liberals for the creation of a new and free German homeland in America: a sizable number of Germans emigrated to Missouri and southern Illinois to carry out these plans. In the 1840's, large tracts of land were bought in Texas by German noblemen and many thousands of German settlers were sent there with the intention of creating a German nation in Texas, or even transforming Texas itself into a German state. A little later a tremendous German migration took place into Wisconsin—and the most perceptive writer on the Germans in America (John Hawgood, *The Tragedy of German America,* 1940) argues that at least some of those involved in fostering it were very likely motivated by the idea of making Wisconsin a German state—and very nearly succeeded. But the net effect of this German effort at nation-building in America was only a few all-German schools, a few all-German towns, which by the third and fourth generation were speaking English and were demanding that the sermons in their churches be given in English.

The Germans in Europe were a nation before they became a state—that is, they existed as a nationally conscious group before the legal form of a German nation was created. The Irish, the second most important element in the earlier immigration, were also a nation before they were a state, and many came to America with the intention of assisting the creation of an Irish state in Europe. On one occasion they did not hesitate to organize armies in America to attack the British in Canada. (Many years later, American Jews were equally unconcerned about sponsoring armed resistance to the same power.) But they did not, as did the Germans, make any serious efforts to create an Irish nation in the full sense of the word in America. In 1818, Irish associations in New York and Philadelphia petitioned Congress for a large tract of land on which to settle Irish poor from the Eastern cities; but there seems to have been no national intention involved. Congress's decision on this occasion settled once and for all the possibility of nationally conscious European nations recreating themselves in America. It refused to sell land in blocks for such purposes, insisting on individual sales and individual settlement. This was certainly one of the most important decisions made in the first half-century of America's national existence.

In any case, it is highly questionable whether national homogeneity, even had Congress approved the Irish request, could have been maintained; in almost every immigrant group individual motives kept on asserting themselves, and again and again caused the disintegration of . . . homogeneous colonies . . . and led the immigrants who had come to settle on the land, with its conservative influences, to desert it for the city, with its powerful assimilative effects. The decision, on the national level, in favor of individual settlement; the decision, on the part of individual settlers, to strike out without the formal assistance of colonies and settlement companies, with their inevitable authority over their settlers—these two facts made it impossible, despite the ideology of the Germans, and of perhaps some Irishmen, to create branches of European nations in America.

A third factor was equally important: the division of labor which took place on the frontier, with English-speaking elements, as the first settlers everywhere, naturally claiming the prerogatives and power of the first-comers. If, like the Mormons, the Germans had struck out into unsettled territory, they would have had a state or states for themselves, with all the power—for example, to determine the official state language—that the Constitution reserves for states. But they never, not even in Wisconsin, had the strength to establish such a state as the Mormons made for themselves in Utah—that belongs to the first-comers. And everywhere the first-comers were Anglo-Saxons. Centuries in the New World had created the highly specialized breed of frontiersman who could do the initial clearing of the wilderness while feeding himself by means of his rifle. . . .

Again and again, it can be seen how the first few thousand settlers in an area had far more weight in . . . [cultural and political life] than hundreds of thousands who came later. They set up the school system; the legal system; they wrote the state constitution; they had the most political experience; they had the prestige which led the later-coming majority—or at least their children—to conform to *their* standards, rather than vice versa.

So while many Germans, and some Irish, came with the intention of creating a "nation of nations," most of them ended up as the principal ingredients of the "melting pot."

Perhaps more successful in creating nations—at least for a while—was what we might call the "intermediate" immigration: the Norwegians and Swedes. . . . The peasants who came to this country from Scandinavia thought of themselves less as members of nations than as coming from a certain family and village, and belonging to a certain church.

Despite this, more of them were successful in creating a national existence in America than were the Germans; that is, they lived in homogeneous farming colonies using their native language, had their own newspapers, books, and publishing houses, a church that conducted its activities in the language of the "old country," and schools to continue the language and culture in succeeding generations. And this was accomplished without the aid of the ideology which moved the Germans: it was accomplished solely by the conditions of their settlement in America. For while there was no need for the Norwegian or Swedish peasant to think of himself as a Norwegian or Swede in the home country—and indeed, he did not—he was immediately faced with the need for establishing his own identity here. He had to consider whether he should send his children to the English school, or set up his own school; whether to attend the English-speaking church, or establish branches of the established church of the old country. And since the natural course of settlement was to seek out the regions where friends and countrymen and relatives had settled, and so to create a dense concentration of settlers clearly marked off from the surrounding countryside, this answer was given by conditions. . . .

Insofar as the Germans settled under the same circumstances, they showed the same history; but the Germans as a group were much more widely distributed, occupationally and geographically, than the Norwegians and Swedes. The Irish, as concentrated geographically as the Scandinavians, lived in the cities, in which an isolated folk existence was impossible, and they were even more dispersed occupationally than the Germans. Eventually, the growth of the cities, the rise of greater attraction there than in farming, and the actual decline of the farming population were the means by which these Scandinavian colonies too were reduced, and these elements too, in sizable measure, entered the melting pot.

It is consequently rather simple-minded to think of the Germans, Irish, Norwegians, and Swedes as groups that easily assimilated to the Anglo-Saxon temper of American life. The Germans in particular had a strong feeling against assimilation. They felt they had brought culture to a relatively benighted country—as, indeed, in certain respects they had. They opposed intermarriage; they felt very strongly about the maintenance of "Germanism." True, they never succeeded in giving really solid institutional form to their feeling for German life and culture, and when World War I came they buried their opposition and quite disappointed the German Government with their American patriotism. . . .

We can, I think, conclude: where these early immigrants were isolated and remained rural, they showed an amazing persistence in maintaining the old language, religion, and culture (or, to be more exact, variants of each, developed in response to American conditions: nothing was transplanted unchanged). Where they settled in cities, as did the Irish, many of the Germans, and the later Norwegians and Swedes, a shorter time sufficed to remove the language and culture they had brought with them.

But this did not end the matter, for after language and culture were gone, ideology and religion remained. The Irish did not live under circumstances that permitted them to construct in America the amazing replicas of the old country that rural settlers were able to create in many other places. They became culturally indistinguishable from their surroundings much faster than if they had become farmers; but they continued to be distinguished by their strong concern for the fate of the old country.

Supporting this concern for the old country in almost every case was the old religion. [For] the state churches of the old country were thrown on the mercy of the immigrants in the new. [See discussion on Churches in "Common Denominators," in this section below.] And these, clutching at everything familiar in the strange new world, supported them as they never would have at home. Religion became, for many groups, indistinguishable from loyalty to the old homeland. (In those cases, as in Poland and Ireland, where the religion of an oppressed national group differed from that of the oppressors, the church had already taken on the character of a national church, linked with the national struggle, that it commonly took on in America.) There was a certain virtue for the immigrant groups in this confusion between religious devotion and national allegiance. For since religion is rigorously separated from American public life, loyalty to the old country in the form of heightened religious practice did not compete in any way, either in the minds of older Americans or of immigrants, with loyalty to America. But despite the honesty with which the immigrant could believe that he had divested himself of all political ties to the homeland, it would be naïve not to see in the religion of many immigrant groups transmuted substitutes for allegiance to the abandoned countries. And indeed, when the mother countries were imperiled, the churches often played a leading role in bringing to their aid the children settled in America.

We can thus, by some oversimplification, distinguish two very distinct sources in the complex of factors preventing the full assimilation of the early immigrant groups: one arose from the conditions of settlement (isolation and concentration); one arose from what we may call ideological commitment to the old country—its religion, its culture, its political and national needs. The Germans were strengthened in their apartness by both; the Irish by the latter; the Norwegians and Swedes, with no country to free from a foreign yoke, only by the former.

The later immigrants showed the same range of variability, with the same, as well as different, factors at work. They also came from nations struggling to become states (Poles, Lithuanians, Slovaks, Croats, Slovenes), states struggling to become nations (Italy, Turkey, and Greece), as well as areas quite outside these Western concepts of state and nation (Syrians); and they included as their second most numerous element, a people—the Jews—who fell into none of these categories completely, but who, almost by dint of their own efforts, created a state and so finally "normalized" themselves. . . .

Yet the newcomers became European nations—and nationalists—in America. . . . Indeed, the creation of national languages, a task which the Western European nations had accomplished centuries before, was considerably facilitated for these backward peoples by American emigration. In American cities people of various villages speaking various dialects came together, and they needed a common, standardized language. [See discussion on Foreign-Language Press and Radio in "Common Denominators," in this section below.] Also they were far more dependent on newspapers than at home—and this required a standardized written language. The first newspaper in the Lithuanian language was published in the United States, not in Lithuania. The urbanization of many East European peoples occurred in America, not ın Europe; and the effects of urbanization—its creation of some common denominator of nationality, its replacement of the sub-ideological feelings of villagers with a variety of modern ideologies—were in large measure first displayed in America. The Erse revival began in Boston, and the nation of Czechoslovakia was launched at a meeting in Pittsburgh. And all this should not surprise us too much when we realize that some of these areas in Europe were so depopulated that the immigrants and their descendants in America sometimes surpassed in numbers—not to speak of wealth—those who were left behind.

If some nations were in large measure created in America, other immigrants were to discover on coming to America that they had left nations behind—nations in which they had had no part at home. Thus, the American relatives of Southern Italians —to whom . . . the Ethiopian war meant nothing more than another affliction visited upon them by the alien government of the North—became Italian patriots in America and supported Mussolini in a war to which they would have been indifferent in Italy.

Nevertheless, and in contrast, it was among these same immigrants that the problem of the violent turning away of the second generation from the life of the first—that intense passion for Americanization whose other side is self-hatred and rejection—became an important phenomenon. When we consider such questions of social psychology, we are not on very sure ground: yet I feel that the problem of the "rejection" of the immigrant parents . . . is the problem of the later immigrant group, not the earlier. And it is not hard to see why. . . . One can understand how it was possible for German culture to maintain itself among such large numbers in the second and third generation— and had it not been for the trauma of the first World War, it would undoubtedly have been much stronger among the third and fourth generations than it is today. For not only could the Germans boast a connection with one of the strongest and most advanced nations in the world; the Americans themselves, up until the first World War, sent their most promising students to study in German universities. In the same way, less important groups like the French and Dutch in America could take pride in their ancestry. And of course the large immigration from Great Britain also had no occasion to forget its past.

How much sadder was the condition of Slovaks and Ruthenians and Croats! . . . They could not even answer the common American question, "What are you?" They were listed in immigration and census statistics indiscriminately as natives of "Austria-Hungary," and they themselves often lacked any clearer notion of who they were than the Americans who dubbed them "bohunks." So while, on the one hand, the conditions of existence in a strange land led them to come together to found newspapers and fraternal societies, and eventually to determine to take pride in their ancestry and some interest in their homelands—at the same time, the fact that they came from nations of peasants, caste nations without an aristocracy or a middle class, and with only the beginnings of an intelligentsia, meant that large numbers of them were unable to define themselves in terms of their origins and therefore flung themselves into a feverish Americanization.

The tragedy of these nationless and past-less immigrants has nowhere been better told than by Louis Adamic . . . himself an immigrant from one of those relatively history-less peoples of the Balkans. . . . He wrote more on this problem than anyone else— though he was as perplexed after he had written five books on the subject as before he wrote the first. He was deeply worried about the second generation arising from a people in whom— as far as they knew—they could take no pride. He found the second generation changing their names and becoming more Americanized in their attachments to fads and surface mannerisms than the "Americans" themselves. They seemed to him utterly empty, rootless, and unreal. . . .

To return to the two concepts with which we began: the "melting pot" described the reality of assimilation which has characterized, to some extent, and in every period, each one of the ethnic groups migrating to this country. The "nation of nations" described one reality for the earlier period of our history: those homogeneous colonies to be found principally on the Great Plains, but to some extent everywhere in the country, which maintained the immigrant's language, religion, and culture. Today the "nations" that make up America no longer find much justification in the maintenance of language, religion, and culture: they are private or subconscious "nations" held together only by a nostalgia which does not dare to become an ideology, a frame of mind which itself has no organic relation to their Old World past but is a reaction to the conditions of twentieth-century America.

What remains most questionable today in this history of assimilation is the status and future prospects of these ghost nations, built around ideologies of support of the home countries, and drawing their real strength from experiences in America which make their elements feel less than full Americans. Whether these empty nations are only given the illusion of a relatively vigorous life by recent developments in Europe, or whether the conditions of American life are not such as to maintain and strengthen them for some time to come: this is something that only the next twenty years can decide.

And yet, however it is decided, it is important to realize that this question concerns the different groups that are involved more than it does the American state as a whole. For the history of the assimilation of ethnic groups in this country, whatever the complexities that have characterized it, is overwhelmingly a history of success, from the point of view of the state. Disloyalty —in the first World War, in the second World War, in the present struggle with communism—has never been a serious problem in this country, and indeed, it has been far less serious than in many countries of a homogeneous stock. Further, it could be powerfully argued that in both world wars an ideology independent of ethnic affiliation—in the first war, socialist pacifism, in the second fascism—played a much greater role in whatever disloyalty there was than any national ties. In the present situation, this is so self-evident as to need no argument.

The problem of assimilation is thus no longer a political one in any significant sense. The complete identification of the overwhelming majority of persons in each group with America in spite of any experiences of discrimination is assured. Rather, the problem of assimilation is now a cultural one, and for each group. In each larger or smaller numbers of people now worry as to what to do about the burden of real and imaginary traditions. Should they embrace it, reject it, select from it? And what of the American environment, formally indifferent to ethnic varieties as it is to religious ones? Does it actually encourage or discourage one or another of these solutions? This whole range of problems in the history of ethnic assimilation is still left open, and is worthy of more thought and study than it has received.

IN DEFENSE OF 100 PER CENT AMERICANISM [2]

In 1919, the American Legion wrote into the preamble of its constitution a pledge. . . . "To foster and perpetuate a 100 per cent Americanism."

The Legion is probably responsible for the fact that the term "100 per cent American" is still current. There has long been pressure to wipe the phrase out of our speech, chiefly through ridicule. The ridicule has been effective. Many Americans cannot say "100 per cent American," except in jest or criticism, without having it stick in their throats. . . .

In fact the words "100 per cent Americanism" and the deeds that express their meaning, have an interesting history.

The word "Americanism" is quite old. It was coined in an attempt to condense into one word the essential differences between American and European culture and forms of government. The differences were real and profound, so the word was a good one. As a catch-word, "Americanism" has always been used with the assumption that the listener knew the marked differences between European and American culture and understood quite clearly what the word meant without further explanation. Thomas Jefferson advised a friend who had spent some time in Europe to return here to live for a while until he had again "become Americanized."

Years later, Edward Bok expressed the same easy understanding of the profound differences between the American and European atmospheres when, in reviewing his career, he titled his autobiography *The Americanization of Edward Bok*.

[2] From "What is 100% Americanism?" by Robert B. Pitkin, managing editor of *American Legion Magazine*. *American Legion Magazine*. 56:24-5+. May 1954. Reprinted by permission.

As the word "Americanism" in its various forms grew, it took on new meanings without losing its older ones. Emerson sometimes used the word to criticize our nineteenth-century "uncultivated" rough-and-readiness. But whether he used "Americanism" in praise or in protest, he used it correctly to indicate the well-understood flavor of American life as it differed from European life.

There came a day, however, when the word "Americanism" dealt with the problem of people who did not know the differences between the American and the European atmospheres. That day dawned with the influx of vast and virtually uncontrolled waves of immigration of Europeans to America, which was at its peak between 1880 and 1920.

Encouraged by a growing American industry that was hungry for cheap labor, United States policy over a period of forty years permitted immigration at a rate that vastly overreached our capacity to assimilate the newcomers into American ways and into an understanding of American life and government. . . .

The frightened and often bewildered strangers to our shores huddled together in little islands of European culture in our cities and industrial centers. Ignorance, poverty, fear and strangeness drew them together. Many of their children went to American public schools which "accommodated" them by giving instruction in their old-country language.

Many of the newcomers listened to political leadership that damned American ways and American government. Often neither the followers nor the leaders had the faintest knowledge of American ways and American government. They thought in terms of the czars, kaisers, kings, emperors, police states and oppressions of Europe. Many a touching story of the fears, perplexities and ignorance with which they started life in America has been told by the immigrants of those days.

A growing populace that was ignorant of American life and the principles of American government was an obvious menace to a nation that plots its course according to the judgments of its people. Yet United States policy permitted the wave of immigration to continue unabated, while little was done to help the new immigrants become assimilated except to blame the situation on the newcomers.

In fact, the numbers and the continued ignorance of the immigrants offered both profit and power to some American interests.

As the aliens were more ignorant of American ways they were more manageable as cheap labor. Often, they were exploited and enslaved by money lenders and did not know how to protect themselves under American law.

Then, too, there was political power to be sought by keeping the strangers in separate groups of "minorities" whom unscrupulous leaders could "champion." In order to pose as "the friends of the Poles" or "the friends of the Italians" or "the friends of the Germans" it was in the interest of many politicians to make sure that the Poles and the Italians and the Germans in America did not start thinking of themselves as Americans.

Demagoguery based on a divided America is not what it used to be, but it is still with us. The modern-day Communists rely heavily upon it. Of the 241 subversive groups on the Attorney General's list today, 109 openly appeal to Old World and religious and racial "minority" ties of modern Americans. Present-day efforts to wipe out the McCarran-Walter immigration control bill are largely organized around appeals to Americans of different European origin to seek an increase in the percentage of their particular Old World stock here. America is pictured as a battleground of Europeans for control, which every group now here except the Indians can win if we return to the wide-open immigration of 1880-1920.

The phrase "100 per cent Americanism" was first used to protest the millions of aliens who lived in America by the time of the first World War without understanding their new country or identifying themselves with it. As early as 1888, the elder Henry Cabot Lodge said: "Let us be done with British-Americans and Irish-Americans and German-Americans, and so on, and all be Americans . . . if a man is going to be an American at all, let him be so without any qualifying adjective."

Before 1920, the problem had become so grave that two Presidents of the United States lashed out unmercifully at the immigrants. Whether Theodore Roosevelt invented the phrase "100 per cent Americanism" or not, he gave the phrase its original currency when he proclaimed: "There can be no 50-50 Americanism in this country. There is room for only 100 per cent Americanism."

If the fiery Roosevelt held the hapless immigrants to blame without analyzing the problem too deeply, so did the sober Woodrow Wilson. Said Wilson on May 6, 1914, in Washington, D.C.: "Some Americans need hyphens in their names because only part of them came over." And in St. Paul, Minnesota, in 1919, he said: "I think the most un-American thing in the world is a hyphen."

Such browbeating of the immigrants probably hurt more than it helped. Neither Roosevelt nor Wilson did very much to help the newcomers become assimilated, or to reduce their flow to the level of the nation's capacity to absorb them as citizens as well as laborers.

At its organizing caucus in St. Louis in 1919, The American Legion pledged itself to foster and perpetuate a 100 per cent Americanism. At that time, the immigration problem was uppermost in the Legion's mind too.

The Legion's first concern, when it adopted Roosevelt's phrase, was that its devotion to 100 per cent Americanism should not dissolve into mere windbag patriotism or "vaporizing," as Lodge had called noisy patriotism. At the top of the list of all the things 100 per cent Americanism means, said the Legion, comes education—formal and informal education in the ideals of citizenship and the facts of American life and government, and exposure of deliberate subversion.

The Ku Klux Klan had used "100 per cent Americanism" as a motto to justify bigoted, masked vigilantism. The Legion stood for law and order, and determined to remedy the Klan's perversion of a patriotic motto.

In November 1919 . . . the Legion's first National Convention . . . adopted an Americanism resolution that read:

We recommend the establishment of a National Americanism Commission of The American Legion, whose duty shall be to endeavor to realize in the United States the basic ideal of this Legion of 100 per cent

Americanism through the planning, establishment and conduct of a continuous, constructive educational system designed to:

(1) Combat anti-American tendencies, activities and propaganda;

(2) Work for the education of immigrants, prospective American citizens and alien residents in the principles of Americanism;

(3) Inculcate the ideals of Americanism in the citizen population, particularly the basic American principle that the interests of all the people are above those of any special interests or any so-called class or section of the people;

(4) Spread throughout the people of the nation information as to the real nature and principles of American government;

(5) Foster the teaching of Americanism in the schools.

What these words meant, particularly what the oft-repeated word "Americanism" meant, would depend upon what the Legion would do about it in the future. Clearly, however, the Legion was conscious of the class-warfare doctrine coming from Russia and the European socialists. It was as clearly aware of the special-interest groups in America who placed their interests in cheap labor and exploitable minorities above their country. And in the fourth paragraph of its first Americanism Resolution the Legion intimated that it had no special Americanism doctrine of its own but would place its faith in a citizenry that would be well educated in the "nature and principles of American government." Above all, the Legion linked Americanism with education. Especially in education aimed at making good citizens. . . .

Much of the early Americanism work of the Legion dealt with immigration and education problems, some of which seem unreal today. Working through its Americanism committees, its legislative committees and its posts, the Legion struck at the roots of the matter. It attacked the wall of strangeness and hostility that stood between aliens and their Americanization, whose first barrier was language. It encouraged and endorsed schools for aliens, and operated many of its own, as it still does. It went out of its way to make naturalization an impressive ceremony where new citizens would be welcomed by older ones.

Within two years, the Americanism Commission could report that at its instigation twenty-five states had passed laws requiring English to be the medium of instruction in all public schools. The 1921 Legion convention offered the support of the Legion to all social organizations looking toward the welfare of the alien, and it offered Legion backing to all schools engaged in educating aliens.

The same convention attacked the "padrone" system that kept laborers in perpetual debt to their employers. It declared war on usurious money lenders and "all individuals whose methods of business result in the practical enslavement of the alien for years, thereby retarding . . . his attainment of citizenship." It called on the government to enforce neglected laws requiring proficiency in the English language and a knowledge of American civics and history as a condition of citizenship.

The Legion itself has run a number of noteworthy naturalization schools for aliens, many of which are still in business. It has as often joined in community-wide naturalization-training and "welcome citizen" projects. Most of these efforts are below the national and state legislative level and are carried on by the respective posts and districts.

All of the Legion's experience in the naturalization field indicates that the baiting of aliens as 50-50 Americans earlier in the century was a mistake. Most aliens yearned to become Americanized, but leadership in Americanism had to come from American citizens. The experience of the program is that for all the new Americans the fires of their ambition to read, write and speak English and to know more about American institutions and responsibilities burn fiercely.

It was because Legionaires knew what 100 per cent Americanism meant to them that they refused to drop the phrase in the face of ridicule.

COMMON DENOMINATORS [3]

Each nationality group which has migrated to the United States has developed a wide variety of organizations to meet the fundamental human needs common to all mankind. His churches

[3] From "Agencies Organized by Nationality Groups in the United States" by Yaroslav J. Chyz, manager of the foreign language press division of the Common Council for American Unity, and Read Lewis, the Council's executive director. *Annals of the American Academy of Political and Social Science.* 262:148-58. March 1949. Reprinted by permission.

and religious organizations enable the newcomer to worship God according to his traditional faith and to enjoy the ritual and the hymns in which he has been reared. Newspapers and periodicals bring him news and needed information in his mother tongue. Fraternal benefit societies provide insurance in case of sickness or death. Singing and educational societies express his artistic and cultural interests. Clubs and lodges reflect his social needs. Political and relief organizations evidence his interest in and concern for his native land.

The nationality groups which came from English-speaking countries became the majority group in the United States and impressed their language and institutions on the new continent. The result has been a tendency to think of the agencies created by English-speaking groups as "American," and of similar developments on the part of other nationality groups as "foreign." Actually, all of them reflect the same basic human needs and are adaptations to American conditions. The fact that "foreign" languages are used in organizations developed by newer nationality groups tends to obscure the fact that the organizations themselves are essentially American and persist even when most of their members are unable to speak the ancestral language.

An Italian Catholic parish in the United States differs from a Catholic parish in Italy in very much the same way that a Protestant Episcopal congregation differs in its structure, scope, and mode of activities from a congregation of the Episcopal Church in England. An American newspaper in the Polish language is as American to a Pole in Warsaw as the New York *Times* is to a Londoner. Even such directly transplanted institutions as the German *Turnvereine* or the Czech *Sokols,* or such ritualistically strict bodies as the Orthodox Jewish congregations or the Russian Orthodox Churches, have developed characteristics and acquired peculiarities which single them out as "American" in the eyes of members of the original organizations.

There are, of course, exceptions to this rule, but they are rare and constantly decreasing. It could not be otherwise. The pattern of American life is so much an outgrowth of American conditions that any organization that wants to survive and develop must fit into it. On the other hand, that pattern offered and still offers so much freedom that it not only makes possible the survival of customs and cultural and social activities of various origins but also encourages the development of new organizational forms in which American and transplanted ways and usages are combined. Fraternal and benefit organizations, for example, which in America are the mainstay of many nationality group activities, have no counterpart in Hungary, Poland, or Slovakia. They are a purely American product.

The agencies organized by nationality groups in the United States may be grouped under three main heads: churches, secular organizations, and foreign-language press and radio. Of course, any rigid classification of agencies according to aims and activities is impossible. A fraternal benefit society may publish a foreign-language newspaper. A parish, or even a whole religious body, may devote a large part of its effort to educational and secular activities, especially those that aim to preserve the coherence of the group.

Churches

Religious bodies are the oldest non-governmental forms of organization among all groups of Americans. Religion motivated the migration to these shores of the Pilgrims and the Quakers, the Scotch Presbyterians and the Belgian Protestants, the Moravian Brethren and the Swiss Mennonites, the French-Italian Waldensians and the Ukrainian Shtundists. Those who came here for other reasons were also for the most part religious people, and one of their first activities as a group was founding a congregation and building and maintaining a house of worship.

The oldest known white religious community in what is now the United States was the Catholic parish in St. Augustine, Florida, established in 1565. Because of their Spanish-Mexican membership and language, the Catholic missions and parishes in the American southwest and in California are the oldest non-English religious organizations in this country. The Dutch Reformed Church in New York, established in 1628, and the Swedish Lutheran congregations, founded among the Swedish settlers in Delaware by Reverend Reorus Torkillus about 1641, appear to be the first non-English Protestant religious communities. The first German Lutheran Church was established in New York in 1648. The first Jewish congregation was organized in Newport in 1658. The first Mennonites came to Pennsylvania in 1683. Moravian Brethren settled in the same colony in 1741. The first Russian Orthodox Church was established in Alaska in 1795. The Panna Maria, Polish Catholic parish in Texas, was founded in 1854. The Finns organized their first Lutheran synod in 1870. The first Greek Catholic Church serving Carpatho-Russians and Ukrainians was organized in 1885.

With the influx of larger numbers of their countrymen, the number of parishes and congregations grew and they began to organize themselves into dioceses, synods, provinces, conventions, and conferences. Numerous splits increased the number of religious bodies.

The oldest and largest single denomination among the non-English-speaking groups is the Catholic Church. . . .

The [*Official Catholic*] *Directory* lists some 2,000 parishes [out of 15,914] as being Armenian, French, German, Polish, Syrian, or of other nationalities and rites. Other sources indicate that at least 2,855 parishes are serving Catholics of Armenian, Assyrian, Belgian, Carpatho-Russian, Chinese, Croatian, Czech, Dutch, French, German, Hungarian, Italian, Lithuanian, Maltese, Polish, Portuguese, Rumanian, Russian, Slovak, Slovene, Spanish (Mexican and Puerto Rican), Syrian, and Ukrainian origin. Most of them are of Roman Catholic rite. A few hundred belong to the Armenian, Byzantine (Greek), Chaldean, Maronite, and Melchite rites. Among those of the Byzantine rite is the Ukrainian diocese having 138 Ukrainian parishes with 307,065 members. The so-called Pittsburgh diocese includes 165 Carpatho-Russian, 15 Hungarian, and 2 Croatian parishes with some 285,652 members. Assuming that these figures are typical, the total number of Catholics belonging to known non-English or nationality parishes exceeds five million. Another five million in all probability belong to nationality parishes although the latter are not identified as such.

Prominent among the characteristics that distinguish these nationality parishes are: (*a*) the use of the native language in all or some sermons and in some church songs; (*b*) certain additional rites and customs, such as the blessing of food before Easter, special Christmas customs, and distinctive marriage rites; (c) the celebration of holidays peculiar to the native country, such as St. Casimir's among the Lithuanians, St. Gennaro's and Our Lady of Mt. Carmel among the Italians, and St. Nicholas' among the Carpatho-Russians. In lay activities these nationality parishes differ from others by celebrations, both religious and secular, commemorating prominent personalities or events in the native country.

The largest Protestant denomination among the nationality groups is the Lutheran Church. Most Americans of Danish, Estonian, Finnish, Icelandic, Latvian, Norwegian, and Swedish descent belong to it. Probably the majority of German-Americans are also Lutherans. There are Lutheran communities among the Hungarians and the Slovaks. The Lutheran Church is organized in some twenty national bodies which differ among themselves on dogmatic or organizational grounds: 2 Danish, 3 Finnish, 5 German, 1 Hungarian, 1 Icelandic, 1 Latvian, 5 Norwegian, 1 Slovak, and 1 Swedish. Altogether, . . . they have 15,443 congregations and . . . [nearly seven million] members.

Next in numbers among the Protestant churches are the Reformed religious bodies, with 3,986 churches. . . . Like the Lutherans, they are split into a number of central organizations: 3 Dutch, 1 German, 2 Hungarian, and 1 Slovak.

Baptist denominations have converts among many nationality groups. In some, special nationality Baptist bodies have been organized, such as the Czechoslovak Baptist Convention, the Hungarian Baptist Union, the Italian Baptist Churches, the Roumanian Baptist Association of North America, the Independent Baptist Church of America (Swedish), and others. Considerable Baptist missionary work is being conducted among the Spanish-speaking groups in the southwest. Various sects of Baptists are represented among the 157 Protestant communities of Japanese-Americans.

The Church of the Brethren and other Brethren bodies, some of them known as Dunker, chiefly of German and Swiss origin, have 4,300 congregations. . . . The Evangelical Church, of Methodist origin, has 1,194 churches. . . . Sixteen Mennonite religious bodies have 1,116 churches among the Pennsylvania Dutch and in other states. The Schwenkfelders and the Amana Church Society in the German group, the Huguenots among the French, the Waldensians with French-Italian membership, the Welsh Calvinistic Methodists who in 1920 joined the Presbyterian Church in the United States of America, and the Bohemian and Moravian Brethren of Iowa and the Evangelical Unity of Moravian and Bohemian Brethren in North America among the Czech-Americans, account for some hundred or more congregations. . . . Dissatisfaction with the Irish domination of the Catholic Church in America brought about the organization of the Polish National Catholic Church, which replaced Latin with Polish in its services and otherwise introduced several reforms. . . . For similar reasons the Lithuanian National Reformed Church . . . was organized.

There are many smaller religious bodies in all the groups, in part the result of internal dissent and in part the result of proselytism by Protestant denominations. These bodies include: the Russian Dukhobors around Detroit and San Francisco; Russian Molokans in California; Old Believers around Pittsburgh; Ukrainian Shtundists in North Dakota; Polish Mariawites; the Armenian Evangelical Church; the Unorganized Italian Christian Churches of America; the Portuguese Evangelical Federation of Churches; the Italian Pentecostal Assemblies of God; the Hungarian and Ukrainian branches of the Assemblies of God; and many similar denominations. While they may not number more than a thousand congregations, these smaller sects suggest the differentiation and dissent which find expression in a free country.

Most Christian immigrants from eastern and southeastern Europe and from the Near East, and their descendants, belong to a group of religious bodies with similar rites which use old Slavonic, Greek, Syriac, and Ukrainian languages in their liturgies and are either independent American religious bodies or are connected with the Eastern Patriarchs of Antioch, Constantinople, or Moscow or with church synods of their respective countries. The present unsettled religious conditions in a large part of eastern Europe have created dissension especially in the Russian

Orthodox Church, with one party favoring submission to the Moscow Patriarchate and the other advocating the creation of a supreme Russian Orthodox hierarchy outside the Soviet Union.

Other Orthodox Churches are the Albanian, Carpatho-Russian, Bulgarian, Greek (Hellenic), Rumanian, Serbian, Syrian, Ukrainian Orthodox, and Ukrainian Orthodox Autocephalous, with a total membership of 728,860 in 880 churches.

Not connected with the above Orthodox Churches are religious groups of Armenians and Assyrians from Iraq and Iran. They have their own ancient churches: Church of Armenians in America (Gregorian) with 35 churches and 18,787 members; Assyrian Jacobite Apostolic Church with 4 churches and 3,100 members; and the Church of the East and of the Assyrians (Nestorian) with 10 churches and 3,000 members.

Jewish congregations are divided into three groups. The Orthodox group claims . . . 2,500 congregations . . . The Conservative groups, organized in the United Synagogues, claim . . . 475 congregations . . . [and] . . . the Reform group 302 . . . In addition there are 500 congregations without affiliation, and also a great number of "Holy Day" congregations which exist only for services on High Holy Days. . . .

Other non-Christian groups include Japanese Buddhists, who have 28 congregations in the United States, 19 of them in California; and Mohammedans, who have their mosques or places of worship in Washington, New York, Detroit, and probably also in San Francisco. The members of their congregations hail chiefly from Albania, Arabia, Egypt, Palestine, Iran, Iraq, Turkey, and Bengal and other parts of India.

The foregoing facts and figures are a convincing proof of the extent and vitality of religious life among nationality groups and of the importance and persistence of their churches. Those already referred to reach a total of some 15 million members in more than 32,500 congregations: 5,092,000 members with 2,855 churches in the Catholic Church; 7,116,443 members with 24,998 churches in the Protestant denominations; 753,747 members in 929 churches in the Eastern Orthodox and other Eastern Churches; and some 2 million members with 3,728 congregations in the different Jewish religious bodies. . . .

While native languages are still used in most churches serving nationality groups, the use of English is becoming more widespread, especially in the Dutch, Danish, Norwegian, Swedish, and Jewish congregations. In the Catholic and even in the Eastern Orthodox churches, English sermons are heard more and more frequently. Social activities in the churches in which second and later generations participate are conducted almost exclusively in English in all groups with the exception of Spanish, French, and some German communities.

This trend toward English does not mean the loss of other nationality characteristics. Church traditions, rites, special holidays, social contacts, and intramarriage keep the church communities together even where the original language may have been changed. Many church activities are directed toward strengthening these internal ties. Parochial primary and secondary schools maintained by nationality churches often teach the native language and make the children acquainted with the culture and history of the group here and abroad. Immigrant clergymen rekindle the group spirit and strengthen the ties with the native country. Special colleges and seminaries in this country educate priests, ministers, and rabbis for service in their denominations. In these schools most subjects are taught in English, but with special attention to the language and culture of the group.

On the other hand, nationality group churches, as well as their central bodies, have developed traits and features which are typical of American church life but often entirely unknown in the "old country." Churches which in the "old country" were either state religions or state-supported have had to learn to exist on the material support of their members. The compulsory religious education has had to give way to voluntary Saturday or Sunday schools. The complete authority of the clergy in all church matters has been shared in varying degrees with lay members, who have freedom to disagree and even to carry their dissension to the point of seceding or forming a rival religious organization. Church activities extend to fields rarely entered by church organizations in other countries—large-scale welfare and charitable work, sports, summer camps, printing and publishing, participation in conferences, and consultations with representatives of other creeds.

Adaptation to new needs and conditions and survival among so many other and often rival denominations, along with maintenance of inherited beliefs and traditions, are proof of the vitality of the religious bodies of nationality groups. Many of them have already become and others are on the way to becoming an integral part of America, part and parcel of the diversity which is so characteristic of American religious life.

Organizations

Fraternal benefit organizations, in which members form local branches, lodges, or assemblies through which they pay monthly dues to a national body for some kind of insurance, are the oldest and most enduring of existing secular organizations in our nationality groups. Originally founded to assure the immigrant a decent burial, they have developed into a network of some 150 national organizations with more than three million members, insurance of about three billion dollars, over half a billion dollars in assets, and varied social activities in more than 31,000 lodges and branches, in all states of the Union. They support schools, museums, homes for the aged, orphanages, sport activities, publications, and adult education, and help their young members to pay for college education. Not all of them, of course, are engaged in all these activities or to equal degree in any of them. Smaller organizations are satisfied with fulfilling their benefit obligations to their members. Some of the largest support colleges or sponsor elaborate historical research relating to the group.

There are a large number of local fraternal organizations in which membership is limited to a particular city or a region. Like national organizations, most of them provide the usual sick benefits. Such local organizations are most numerous in the Jewish group, where they take the form of *Landsmannschaften* (societies of people from the same town or region in the native country) but also occur frequently among the German, Greek, and French groups, especially on the west coast, and also in the

Scandinavian (Norwegian *bygdelag*) and some Slavonic groups.

Not a few national and some local fraternal organizations either publish or subsidize newspapers or publications. Eleven dailies, over fifty semiweeklies and weeklies, and about the same number of monthlies are supported in this way.

Several fraternal organizations do not carry insurance benefits, but are active chiefly in social, philanthropic, cultural, and educational fields. The largest Jewish organization—B'nai B'rith, established in 1843—has some 305,000 members in its 900 lodges and 580 chapters, helps Jews abroad, provides educational and social opportunities for its youth, and works for better understanding between Americans of Jewish and other faiths. The Order of the Sons of Italy in America unites some 125,000 members in 940 lodges for social purposes, for promotion of interest in Italian culture, and for organized participation in American life. The American Hellenic Educational Progressive Association (AHEPA) endeavors to integrate Greek and American cultures, while the Greek American Progressive Association (GAPA) is more interested in preserving Greek traditions and languages. The Federation of French Alliances in the United States and Canada maintains and propagates French culture and ideas in America.

Numerous singing societies cultivate and perpetuate native music among the German, Swiss, Swedish, Welsh, Norwegian, Russian, Ukrainian, and other groups. Almost every community with a large "foreign" population has local baseball, basketball, or soccer teams of "foreign" extraction. Jewish "Maccabees" compete with Slovak "St. Mary's," and Armenian "St. Gregory's" play against "Ukrainian Cossacks." The German *Turnvereine* and the Czech and Slovak *Sokols* unite physical culture with the maintenance of their group culture and ideals.

Japanese, Czech, Jewish, Finnish, and other farmers, Kosher butchers, German grocers, French cooks, Italian barbers, Russian lawyers and doctors, Swedish engineers, Norwegian seamen, Lithuanian organists, and other occupational and professional groups maintain local and regional associations of their own. There are associations to further folk dancing and to promote a study of a group's history in America. The American Scandi-

navian Foundation, the Carl Schurz Foundation, the Polish American Historical Commission of the Polish Institute of Arts and
Sciences, the Menorah Society, the Swiss American Historical
Society, the Finnish Suomi College, the Swedish American Bio-
graphical Society, and other similar institutions have made valuable contributions to the historical studies relating to their respective groups.

Organized political activity on a national scale in the domestic field among nationality groups has always been and still is
limited almost exclusively to the left-wing parties. This is partly
due to the fact that many so-called "radical" ideas have been
transplanted into America from abroad, and partly because the
leftist parties look for recruits among American workers, so many
of whom are of recent immigrant stock. In the past, the Socialist
Party, the Industrial Workers of the World, the Socialist Labor
Party had large nationality "federations" or "sections." Some of
them survive. At the present time [1949] the Communist Party
of America is the most active in the nationality field, with various
nationality sections of the fraternal International Workers Order
as the main lever of its activities. Participation in other parties
is organized through local "Polish" or "Italian" Republican or
Democratic clubs, with an occasional state league or federation
of such clubs.

In the foreign field, on the other hand, the activities of
nationality groups are much more vigorous and diversified, especially among immigrants from central and eastern Europe. Unsettled conditions in some countries, sharp division of opinion
regarding existing regimes, and efforts by political parties abroad
have stimulated among the politically minded members of various groups interest and activities relating to the "old country,"
to an extent which some outside observers consider excessive.
Actually, such interest and activities, in most cases, are limited
to sharp articles in the foreign language press, a few conventions and resolutions, memoranda and delegations to administration and congressional leaders in Washington, and some financial
help to the kindred groups and leaders abroad. Often these
political interests and activities bring to the closer attention of
our Government and the American public many urgent issues on

which the United States must sooner or later take action. Information services issued by various nationality groups frequently contribute material which helps America to make up its collective mind on important international issues. In fact, one can only regret that this material is not more fully explored and utilized.

Charitable and welfare activities for the benefit of the needy members of one's group played a much more prominent part in the life of immigrants in the past than they do now. Fraternal benefit organizations resulted from such concern. At the present time several orphanages, more numerous homes for the aged, and a few hospitals and homes for the blind or crippled comprise the total of such activities. They are most numerous in the Jewish group. Otherwise, needy members of nationality groups must turn for help to general private and public agencies. On the other hand, activities for aid to kinsmen abroad have increased during and since World War II. Hundreds of millions of dollars are collected annually. All nationality groups have special committees for various forms of help to their kinsmen in other parts of the world. Many of them are members of the American Council of Voluntary Agencies for Foreign Service or have joined CARE—Cooperative for American Remittances to Europe, Inc.

The passage of the Displaced Persons Act of 1948 is directing the activities of Croatian, Czech, Estonian, German, Hungarian, Jewish, Latvian, Lithuanian, Polish, Russian, Serbian, Slovak, and Ukrainian relief organizations to the task of bringing their kinsmen to America and finding homes and employment for them. In the case of larger groups the task is not too difficult; but small American groups with large numbers of prospective immigrants, such as Estonians, Latvians, and to a degree Ukrainians, must turn to religious organizations for help to carry on this work.

Foreign-Language Press and Radio

Der Hoch-Deutsche Pennsylvanische Geschicht-Schreiber, which made its appearance in Philadelphia in 1739, was the sixth American periodical and came into existence only thirty-five years after the first American newspaper, the Boston *News-Letter.*

From that time on, the press in German and later in other languages grew until it reached its peak during the First World War with more than 1,350 publications in 36 languages. At the end of July 1948 there were 973 publications in 40 languages. . . .

Almost all of the [current] 95 non-English dailies and about 40 per cent of the 37 semiweeklies, 374 weeklies, and 467 periodicals are owned by individual publishers or by small corporations or partnerships. The rest are owned by religious, fraternal, or cultural organizations. They range all the way from small, struggling sheets printed and edited by a single individual to influential weeklies and large dailies, with circulation running into six figures, equipped with modern plants and capable of producing impressive Sunday editions.

All the dailies and 337 of the 411 weeklies and semiweeklies are newspapers in the strict sense of the word. In addition to carrying general news and editorials, some of them at the same time serve as organs of fraternal organizations. Depending chiefly on individual subscriptions or on organization support, foreign-language papers reflect the views of their readers much more closely than many of their English-language counterparts, which derive most of their income from advertising.

Almost two hundred foreign-language publications are the organs of religious organizations, and some three hundred are purely fraternal publications or are issued by political groups, cultural agencies, or trade interests. About forty Spanish and Portuguese publications which, though published in the United States, circulate chiefly in Latin America fall in the last group.

As to content, foreign-language newspapers naturally devote most space to news about the "old country" or to events in their own group. At the same time, they carry a considerable amount of material on the American scene. Throughout its history, the foreign-language press has served as a sort of textbook and guide to American customs and institutions, American history, government, naturalization, and the thousand and one things a newcomer wants and needs to know in order to adjust himself to his American environment. . . . In general, foreign-language newspapers encourage their groups to preserve their cultural heritage, religion, language, and social customs, and yet, at the same time, to find their place in the American community and participate in American life. . . .

Supplementing the foreign-language press, but of much less importance as a means of reaching the nationality groups in the country, are the more than 300 foreign-language radio programs which in 1948 were being broadcast each week in twenty-six different languages. These programs were broadcast from more than 125 different stations, located in some twenty-six states. Approximately 10 per cent of the programs are sponsored by religious groups, another 10 per cent by fraternal organizations, and the remaining 80 per cent are commercial undertakings aimed at the foreign-language market in a given locality.

In many cases the foreign-language broadcaster is connected with a local foreign-language newspaper. He usually buys a block of time from a local station and sells as much time as possible to local advertisers. The result is that most foreign-language programs are isolated units and, with notable exceptions, are disrupted by an overdose of commercials. While some stations have included features of outstanding cultural and educational value, most programs consist chiefly of music, news, entertainment features, and comment, which are supposed to appeal to different tastes and different sections of nationality groups.

As Affecting Assimilation

Do the agencies organized by American nationality groups— their churches, organizations, press—aid or hinder assimilation? The question, however interesting, is in a sense academic, for such agencies are an inevitable result of large-scale immigration. If America had not given the newcomer the freedom to organize, to express and pursue his interests, it would neither have been America nor have attracted the millions of immigrants who have come here. Further, even as cursory a survey of nationality group agencies as has been possible in this article suggests they are here to stay, a permanent part of American life; that their apparent differences from the accepted "American pattern" are no greater than those shown once by the Quakers of Pennsylvania or the Mormons of Utah. Use of foreign languages will gradually in most cases give way to English, but most of the organizations, both religious and secular, will persist.

Do such agencies aid or hinder assimilation? The answer depends in part on what one means by "assimilation." If it spells loss of all group identity and unconditional acceptance of the language, customs, religious beliefs, and cultural patterns of New England, the "deep South," the West or Middle West— depending on where the newcomer happens to be settled—then these agencies must be counted an obstacle to assimilation. But if the essence of assimilation is, first of all, emotional identification with America and second, participation in general American life, if assimilation is considered not a one-way process but a mutual adjustment, then these agencies must be regarded as instruments of individual and group adjustment to America.

Agencies organized by a nationality or any other group naturally place a certain emphasis on the things—in this case, common heritage and language—which are the basis of the group's existence. To some extent, consequently, they tend to increase group consciousness as contrasted with emotional identification with America. It must be remembered, however, that most of these same agencies have been founded to meet the immigrant's needs in a new country. In a deeper sense, therefore, they are instruments of his adjustment and have a profound influence in furthering his assimilation. They facilitate, rather than prevent, his participation in such general American activities as trade unions and political parties and in local community affairs. Even the emphasis on native language and culture is likely in the end to enrich and strengthen America and equip it better for its historic task of forging a united and peaceful world.

PUERTO RICAN IN-MIGRATION [4]

When the big waves of immigration began in the middle of the last century, it became pretty much the rule that the bottom-of-the-ladder jobs in the labor market were filled by newcomers.

[4] From "Puerto Ricans Start up Labor Ladder." *Business Week.* p 150-2. May 2, 1953. Reprinted by special permission from *Business Week,* a McGraw-Hill publication. Copyright 1953 by McGraw-Hill Publishing Company.

As each group adapted itself to American society and worked up, another was ready to take its place at the bottom. But with the passage of restrictive immigration laws in the 1920's, the major influx from Europe ended.

Now, a new group is starting at the bottom in New York and other cities and is gradually moving up and out into the economy. The group this time is the Puerto Ricans. Strictly speaking, they are not immigrants. The correct word is "migrants," because they are native-born American citizens, free to come and go as they please without restriction by immigration quotas.

The wave of migration from Puerto Rico that began early in World War II and burgeoned after the war has probably brought more than 400,000 people to the mainland and promises to bring still more. Since the Puerto Ricans don't show up as immigration statistics, all figures about their numbers are at best informed guesses. It is generally believed that [by 1953] there . . . [were] more than 375,000 in the New York area with a scattering elsewhere. Chicago probably has upwards of 15,000, the Philadelphia-Camden area maybe 5,000, Lorain, Ohio, another 4,500, and so on through the eastern half of the country and to a lesser extent in the West.

Most of the Puerto Ricans are employed in manufacturing and service industries, though some hold white-collar and professional positions, especially in New York City. There are perhaps 20,000 in New York's garment industry and about 16,000 in hotels and restaurants. They work in foundries in Milwaukee and Bridgeport, steel mills in Lorain and Youngstown.

Employers agree that they are as industrious as any other ethnic group and as physically and mentally competent. Their education level seems to be as high or higher, and many have skills acquired on the island.

Different customs and language create their biggest adjustment problems. But given the opportunity and a little English, employers and social workers agree, they learn the ropes fast. Puerto Rican representatives say language difficulties often give unscrupulous landlords and employers a chance to exploit the Puerto Ricans.

The Commonwealth of Puerto Rico itself neither encourages nor discourages migration of its people to the mainland. However, it takes the position that since many are going to migrate, the government ought to let them know what they are in for and give them a hand in adjusting when they get to the mainland.

To carry out this policy, the migration division of the Puerto Rican Labor Department was set up in March 1948, when annual migration passed the 25,000 mark. Headed by Clarence Senior, social scientist and Latin American expert, the division has local offices in New York and Chicago. These offices serve as a cushion between the newcomers and their adjustment problems.

As affiliates of the United States Employment Service, these offices locate jobs for any Puerto Ricans who choose to use them. They work with employers, showing them how they can help the new employees fit in more quickly. The offices cooperate with social agencies and encourage them to provide social and cultural activities—aimed at smoothing the fitting-in process.

The local labor offices require that prevailing labor standards be met before they will accept an order for workers. And though the division maintains strict neutrality in labor organizing drives, it cooperates with already organized unions in providing interpreters and other services wherever it feels that this will protect and improve labor standards of the migrants.

One of the biggest jobs of the migration division is dispelling myths about Puerto Rico and its people that sometimes result in discrimination and tensions in areas where the islanders have settled. Officials of the division maintain that despite the belief in some quarters that migration stems from attempts by the island government to export its poverty, the migrants have more education and skills than the average for the island. It has even been suggested that the island government would like to discourage some of the migration because local industry is losing too much skilled labor.

The biggest long-term problems that most communities face in handling the migrants are housing and recreation facilities. New York's difficulties have been well documented, and they are different from those of smaller cities. But Bridgeport, with about five thousand Puerto Ricans, presents a typical example of what other areas will face as more and more migrants spread out from New York.

On the outside, many of the homes in Bridgeport's Puerto Rican section look like the old one-family and two-family houses they once were. But landlords have converted many of them into high-rent, pint-sized apartments and furnished rooms, so that buildings that once housed eight or ten people now rent to forty or more.

In some cases lack of housing has even created labor problems. At H. O. Canfield Company, mechanical rubber producers, a personnel official who expressed great satisfaction with the 80 Puerto Ricans employed by the company complained that poor housing has caused absenteeism. Some of his employees who can't find places for their families in Bridgeport have left them in New York. They go down for visits on weekends and occasionally miss Monday morning shifts.

The absence of recreational facilities also makes for problems among Puerto Rican workers in Bridgeport. A movie that shows Spanish-language films, a few bars, and a restaurant provide just about all the entertainment available to Puerto Ricans. What's more, the unwillingness of many of the more integrated and successful Puerto Ricans to have much to do with the newcomers has made it difficult for the new settlers to find a bridge between island customs and mainland ways of living.

Most of the migrants now on the continent seem anxious to stay. About 95 per cent of the men and more than half of the women—many in domestic service—are gainfully employed. Of the 5 per cent on relief in New York City, more than three fourths are women with dependent children. Few come along just for the ride from the island. Most follow friends and relatives who have already lined up jobs for them.

THE PUERTO RICAN PROBLEM IN NEW YORK [5]

New York is a city of prodigious problems. One of its greatest is what New York slums are doing to American citizens from Puerto Rico.

[5] From article by Blake Clark, roving editor of *Reader's Digest*. *Reader's Digest*. 62:61-5. February 1953. Reprinted by permission.

From 1908 to 1945, only about 2,200 Puerto Ricans a year came to the States and stayed. But in 1946, with unrestricted postwar air transportation, forty thousand dug up passage to the promised land. Since then, some 230,000 more have joined them and they are now pouring in at the rate of sixty thousand a year in the greatest air migration in history. Already, every tenth Manhattan Island resident is Puerto Rican.

From arriving planes at New York airports step little women clad only in cotton dresses, even in midwinter, and men with no coats to protect them against the freezing wind. Many find shelter in the crowded, crumbling tenements of the city's Spanish Harlem, where their poverty and inadequate English imprison them.

Here merchants charge them exorbitantly for their food and every other necessity bought on credit. Low-price chain stores do not accept charge accounts; competition ceases to operate for people who must have credit before the end of every month. Landlords, too, victimize them pitilessly. The ceiling rental on a typical four-bedroom unfurnished apartment is $38 a month. Putting in a few pieces of second-hand paraphernalia, the owner converts it to four furnished rooms with one bath and kitchen for all, each room bringing $60 a month. At this rate, frequently an entire family must live in one room. . . .

Even worse are hundreds of condemned basements and cellars into which landlords crowd families, gouging them for standard apartment rates. In one I visited, five families were holed up in cubicles that were formed by flimsy partitions. In another, each person must wait his turn with seventeen others to reach the single toilet. A woman in one of these burrows kept a mop constantly at hand to fight the water that dripped from an overhead pipe. "Super [the superintendent] just say, 'Me no feex notheeng,' " she explained to me.

The end results of such an existence are what you might expect: disease, delinquency and crime. . . .

While Puerto Ricans constitute one tenth of the Manhattan population, it has been estimated that they account for more than one sixth of the crimes. Among 11,343 persons who in 1951 were arraigned in Felony Court, Manhattan, 1,750 were Puerto Ricans; so were 583 of the 2,407 adolescents brought into Youth

Term Court. Of the 1,006 prostitutes arraigned in six months, 178 were Puerto Rican.

The tragedy is that the majority of Puerto Ricans are fundamentally warm-hearted, courageous, and eager to make their way in the land they rightfully regard as theirs. Many are making a valuable contribution in business, industry and the arts. About twelve thousand work at skilled jobs in the garment industry, and thousands of others are employed in radio-assembly plants, pharmaceutical laboratories, blanket factories, paper companies and a dozen other industries where they average $40 to $75 a week. These hard-working, quiet newcomers are steadily raising the level of New York's employment pool.

Over a hundred work in Howard Johnson's seventeen New York restaurants, where they are found to be generally "clean, competent and dependable." The personnel director of the Waldorf-Astoria declares that his hotel now depends upon the islanders to a great extent in the steward's department. "We've tried others," he says, "but few have the stick-to-itiveness of the Puerto Ricans." Probably 75 per cent of the busboys, dishwashers, pot-and-pan cleaners and other behind-the-scenes workers who keep the city's dining rooms going are Puerto Ricans.

Ambitious Puerto Ricans by the thousands study English at night. In 1951, eleven thousand attended courses in settlement-house classrooms and public night schools. The cheering fact that so many not only make the best of a bad lot but are actually forging ahead is a testament to human resilience, and proof that others can lift themselves, too.

Unfortunately, the colony's situation seems bound to get worse as long as nearly a thousand islanders a week continue to fly in. The problem is housing. In New York, dwellings are deteriorating faster than they are being replaced. Builders would have to put up more than 130,000 new units a year to provide adequate housing for New Yorkers by 1963. Actually they are building about 35,000. The major deterrent to faster building is high construction costs. Most Puerto Ricans can afford to pay about $9 a month rent per room; but the lowest construction costs demand a return of at least twice that. "New York housing used to be deplorable," said one official. "Now it's hopeless."

What can be done? The best course for incoming Puerto Ricans would be to skip the overcrowded metropolis and head for the hinterland. If more would push on westward, most of their problems — and some of New York's — would disappear. Some 15,000 in Chicago, 4,000 in Bridgeport, Connecticut, 3,000 in Lorain, Ohio, 2,500 in Philadelphia, and lesser numbers in other cities not only enjoy as high wages as their countrymen in New York but are more comfortably housed, in better health and rarely on relief. They still tend to group together, since only about half arrive in the States with a knowledge of English, but they enjoy a good reputation with the police, the business community, labor unions and the church.

The islanders will go wherever they can find jobs. The Migration Division of the Puerto Rican Department of Labor sends field laborers to summer employment in fruit orchards and vegetable farms, where they are needed. Four thousand were flown to Michigan in ten days, and saved a $14 million sugar-beet crop.

Seventy-six pioneering Puerto Ricans and their families are happily settled in Bingham Canyon, Utah, where the men mine copper. Beginning as day laborers, in six years they have mastered the most complicated phases of this industrial operation and average some $6000 a year—about the same as a member of the Puerto Rican governor's cabinet received a few years ago.

I first came to know and like Puerto Ricans in their homeland. There are no finer people than the cultivated, well-adjusted groups to be found on the island. They are intelligently aware of their local problems and are attacking them with courage and imagination. A few thousand study in colleges and graduate schools in the United States each year, returning to Puerto Rico to useful, often brilliant, careers in the professions, business and the arts. They are a most desirable type of American.

The vast majority of those who come here naturally lack these advantages. Like millions of other Americans before them, these plucky people are at the bottom of the occupational pyramid. Denned up in the slums, they are under terrific pressure. Under these conditions, and with still more immigrants arriving every week, the problem continues to be a most serious one for New York. But those who work closest with the Puerto Ricans believe that eventually they can be assimilated throughout the country. Chief Magistrate John M. Murtagh remarks: "Don't forget—in our time we Irish gave New York a few headaches, too."

IMMIGRATION AND AMERICA'S STRENGTH [6]

Viewing the present position of the United States in the light of unbiased historical judgment, it is evident that our rapid rise to world power has been based on an enormous increase in population during the past 175 years. In that period, our numbers went from some four million to more than 150 million people. This tremendous growth was largely the result of immigration. In 1940, for example, it was estimated that of the total white population of 118.2 million, 67.9 million were of later immigrant stock (i.e., descendants of persons coming to the United States after 1789). Only 50.3 million were descendants of early immigrant stock (i.e., descendants of persons coming to the United States before 1789).

The contribution of the immigrant to American economic, intellectual and spiritual life has been often recounted. In terms of manpower, organizing ability, inventive genius, and advancement of the arts and sciences he has contributed much to the building of America.

From the earliest days of the Republic, the immigrant helped to create employment by introducing new industries. The chemical industry was introduced into Delaware by the French. The Swiss and French were the first watchmakers. Tanning was introduced by the Germans; the glove industry by the Scotch. The clothing industry was founded here by the Germans, Austrians, Russians and Italians. The wine industry in this country was largely the work of Italian immigrants.

Without the manpower supplied by immigration, the process of industrial growth and development would have been long delayed. The German, Scandinavian, and southern European

[6] From *Paths To The New World: American Immigration—Yesterday, Today and Tomorrow*, by Edward Corsi, state government official and former United States Immigration Commissioner. (Freedom Pamphlet Series) Anti-Defamation League of B'nai B'rith. 212 Fifth Avenue. New York 10. 1953. p 15-23. Reprinted by permission.

groups followed the pioneers westward to cultivate the undeveloped land. The railroads were pushed toward the Pacific by the work of the Irish, the Poles, the Italians, while in the far west the Chinese lent a hand. Coal was dug and iron ore mined by the Hungarians, the Poles, and other immigrants from Central Europe. Much of the work that went into our highway system, our canals and our shipbuilding was performed by immigrant labor. The great expansion of American industry that took place in the last decades of the nineteenth and the early part of the twentieth century would have been impossible without the muscles and the brains of new Americans.

Many immigrants played outstanding roles in promoting progress in later stages of the country's development. For instance: Andrew Carnegie (steel), John J. Bausch and Henry Lomb (optical goods), Michael Cudahy (meat packing), Charles Fleischmann (yeast), David Sarnoff (radio), Frederick Weyerhaeuser (lumber), and William S. Knudsen (automobiles). In the fields of science, invention and the arts the contributions of the immigrant have been equally great. Among the intellectual giants whose genius has benefited America may be mentioned Enrico Fermi (Italy) and Albert Einstein (Germany), both of whom made essential contributions in the field of atomic energy. Charles Steinmetz (Germany), and Michael Pupin (Serbia) in the field of electricity, and Selman Waksman (Russia) in the field of medicine. Among the inventors are such names as John Ericsson (Sweden) who invented the screw propeller, Giuseppe Bellanca (Italy) who contributed to airplane development, John A. Udden (Sweden) who was responsible for opening the Texas oil fields, Lucas P. Kyrides (Greece) who made important advances in industrial chemistry, and Alexander Graham Bell (Scotland) who invented the telephone.

The field of serious music would lose much of its luster without such men as Arturo Toscanini, Fritz Kreisler and Jascha Heifetz. Most of our more important opera singers are either immigrants themselves or the descendants of immigrants. In popular music, many of the tunes which America sings are the work of such immigrants as Irving Berlin and Victor Herbert. Among our foreign born men of letters have been such names as Morris Raphael Cohen and Hendrik Van Loon. The great newspaper publisher Joseph Pulitzer was an immigrant. . . .

There are few today who would urge that this country should return to the free immigration that characterized the first century of the nation's history. Free immigration does not differentiate between desirable persons and those who are unacceptable by reason of health, morals, or criminality or other anti-social activities. It does not permit selection on the basis of the needs of the American economy. Nor does it consider our capacity to absorb, which may differ in times of prosperity and depression. It may create difficulties in assimilating new arrivals if large numbers should come within a short space of time. In general, unregulated immigration is inadequate to meet the complex needs of our highly specialized economy.

Most people will agree that the permitted immigration should be restricted as to numbers, selective as to quality, and planned to meet the varying needs of the domestic economy. The question still remains: How many immigrants should be admitted?

A satisfactory answer to this question involves consideration of population trends in the country. It also involves consideration of our capacity to absorb new peoples, taking account of present and future manpower needs. And it implies a definite point of view concerning the future growth of our country.

Population experts point out that our rate of population increase is declining. Although the peak of population is still some time to come, they say, eventually, barring immigration, there will be a downturn in total numbers. They also point out that the average age of the population is gradually increasing. The inevitable result is that in the future we will have more older people who must be supported by persons of working age. Moreover, the ratio of women to men, which throughout our history has favored men, is now shifting so that in the future we will have a preponderance of women.

A marked decline in the rate of population increase will have profound effects on our economic structure, making difficult the maintenance of a free enterprise system. Under such conditions: investment in production tends to drop off, unemployment tends to rise, the demand for agricultural and capital goods declines, investment risks increase, the standard of living is lowered, and the basis for the free enterprise system is undermined.

Projections of our present population (assuming an average number of births and deaths and no *net* immigration) indicate that with no annual net immigration at all after July 1, 1952, in 1960 the population will reach 169.4 million. If a net annual immigration of, say, a half-million annually is assumed during this period, there will be 173.7 million people. Of these, 4.3 millions represent immigrants and their children, an increase of about 2.5 per cent resulting from the immigration. The small impact of this number of immigrants, somewhat larger than most recent proposals have suggested as appropriate, may be judged by the effects of recent internal migrations. One state alone, California, had a population increase of some 4 million in the period from 1940 to 1950. Of this number, 2.6 million represented in-migration from other states. As a result this state has grown economically and culturally.

An annual immigration of this size would have the effect of postponing the population decline predicted by the experts previously quoted. It would also add needed population during the rest of the century. This is especially important in that by the end of the century, without such immigration, we may be expected to have a considerably smaller population than we now have, compared with the USSR and the countries of the Soviet orbit.

Can the American economy absorb as many as 500,000 immigrants annually?

The history of our country has been one of dynamic expansion. The productive capacity of the nation is rising rapidly today, perhaps as rapidly as in any period in our history. Our standard of living is the highest in the world. In the past twenty years our production has risen five times as fast as our population. The inventive genius of the American people, applied to the still under-utilized natural resources of the nation, provides limitless horizons for the future. Increased farm production, utilizing techniques already known, would be sufficient to provide an adequate supply of food for the maximum population that the country is likely to attain. . . .

Except for brief periods of recession, the expanding economy of this nation has always had a need for additional manpower. This need has been met through natural population growth, immigration, and internal shifts of the population.

The labor force increased from 41.2 million in 1920 to 66 million in 1951. If it were not for the restrictive legislation enacted at that time, immigration would have filled a portion of the labor demand, permitting a greater expansion than actually took place. With the curtailment of immigration, the labor demand was met by draining manpower off the farm, by increasing immigration from Puerto Rico and nonquota Western Hemisphere countries, and by importing temporary labor from neighboring lands. Most authorities agree that there is presently an acute shortage of manpower in agriculture and that additional workers can be used by our expanding industry. They point out that all those normally in the labor force are already fully employed. In this connection it should be remembered that in 1950 there were two million fewer young people in the 10 to 19 age group than in 1940, a decrease of 8 per cent. As a result, the annual flow of young workers into the labor force is currently at the lowest point in many years. It will continue low until the larger numbers of children born after 1940 reach working age.

Another indication of our manpower shortage is the lack of available young people to supply the armed forces. This is especially important in the light of the great superiority in numbers enjoyed by the forces of totalitarianism. In addition, in the event of all-out war, we will have many fewer people to draw on than in the last war to man the machines on the home front. . . . Of course, some war manpower needs can be met by shifting workers now employed in normal production to defense production. To the labor force can be added young persons, women, and older persons not normally employed. That is what we did in the last war. The unresolved question is: Will this be sufficient to meet the needs of a new war economy?

If as many as 500,000 immigrants are admitted annually, will this lead to increased unemployment?

In the entire history of our country there is no evidence that unemployment was caused by immigration. In this connection it is important to note that successive waves of immigration have come to the United States in response to both the needs of this country and conditions abroad. Each wave has been a passing phenomenon, rising in amplitude at certain stages of economic and political life and subsiding thereafter. The crests of these waves have invariably come in prosperous times and the shallows in depression or war periods. In fact, during depression periods, the numbers of those leaving America have been much greater than the numbers of those coming to it. From 1932 to 1936, for example, there were approximately 136,000 more departures than there were admissions.

Careful studies have shown that in a growing nation immigration has had little effect on the volume of unemployment, on per capita income, and on wages. These investigations concluded that there was no correlation between the percentage of foreign born in individual states and the percentage of unemployed workers at various periods for which such calculations were made. There was a striking correspondence between the states in which high per capita income existed and in which there were a high proportion of immigrants and new foreign stock. It is also pointed out that this country has always had immigration, yet we have had constantly rising wage levels and an improved standard of living.

That this should be so is not surprising. Immigrants are consumers as well as producers. Half of the immigrants are women and children who do not go into the labor force. When an adult immigrant arrives he adds to the economy the equivalent of a capital investment of perhaps $10,000 which the country of emigration has invested in raising and educating him from childhood. Many bring with them skills and experience which enable them to give employment to others. There is no question, however, that this country can more easily absorb more immigrants in times of prosperity than in times of depression.

In this discussion, an immigration quota of 500,000 per year has been used for illustration. A total immigration of this size would be about one quarter of one per cent of our population and would be well within the capacity of the nation to absorb it.

III. THE McCARRAN-WALTER ACT

EDITOR'S INTRODUCTION

After lengthy hearings and extended debate the McCarran-Walter Act—named for its sponsors in the Senate and House respectively; the late Pat McCarran, Democrat, of Nevada and Francis E. Walter, Democrat, of the Twentieth District of Pennsylvania—was passed by the Eighty-second Congress, and made law over the President's veto on June 27, 1952, by the required two-thirds majority of both houses; in the Senate by 57 votes to 26, in the House by 278 to 113. Three days later the President issued the following proclamation:

A PROCLAMATION

Whereas under the provisions of Section 201 (b) of the Immigration and Nationality Act, the Secretary of State, the Secretary of Commerce, and the Attorney General, jointly, are required to determine the annual quota of any quota area established pursuant to the provisions of Section 202 of the said Act, and to report to the President the quota of each quota area so determined; and

Whereas . . . [they] jointly have made the determination provided for . . . and have fixed, in accordance therewith, immigration quotas as hereinafter set forth:

Now, therefore, I, Harry S. Truman, President of the United States of America . . . do hereby proclaim and make known that the annual quota of each quota area hereinafter enumerated has been determined in accordance with the law to be, and shall be, as follows:

Afghanistan	100	Cameroun	100
Albania	100	Ceylon	100
Andorra	100	China (and other Chinese)	205
Arab Peninsula	100	Czechoslovakia	2,859
Asia-Pacific triangle	100	Danzig	100
Australia	100	Denmark	1,175
Austria	1,405	Eire	17,756
Belgium	1,297	Egypt	100
Bhutan	100	Estonia	115
Bulgaria	100	Ethiopia	100
Burma	100	Finland	566
Cambodia	100	France	3,069
Cameroons	100	Germany	25,814

Greece	308	Pakistan	100
Hungary	865	Palestine	100
Iceland	100	Philippines	100
India	100	Poland	6,488
Indonesia	100	Portugal	438
Iran (Persia)	100	Romania	289
Iraq	100	Ruanda-Urundi	100
Israel	100	Samoa	100
Italy	5,645	San Marino	100
Japan	185	Saudi Arabia	100
Jordan	100	Somaliland	100
Korea	100	Southwest Africa	100
Laos	100	Spain	250
Latvia	235	Sweden	3,295
Lebanon	100	Switzerland	1,698
Liberia	100	Syria	100
Libya	100	Tanganyika	100
Liechtenstein	100	Thailand	100
Lithuania	384	Togo	100
Luxembourg	100	Togoland	100
Monaco	100	Trieste	100
Morocco	100	Turkey	225
Muscat	100	U. of S. Africa	100
Nauru	100	U.S.S.R.	2,697
Nepal	100	United Kingdom	65,361
Netherlands	3,136	Vietnam	100
New Guinea	100	Yemen	100
New Zealand	100	Yugoslavia	933
Norway	2,364		
Pacific Islands	100	Total	154,657

In witness whereof, I have hereunto set my hand and caused the seal of the United States of America to be affixed. . . .

HARRY S. TRUMAN

By the President
   David Bruce
     Acting Secretary of State

The law, by its own provision, became effective on the December 24th following—Christmas Eve.

As President Truman pointed out in his veto message [see below] the McCarran-Walter Act is a long and complex piece of legislation, but considering its own generous provisions, the great number of nonquota immigrants admitted from abroad and from countries in this hemisphere, and our long and practically unguarded borders with Mexico and Canada [see Section I] it seems little more than a Maginot Line, and as likely to be bypassed. It has been controversial, however, since its introduction into Congress, and will undoubtedly be a political issue as long as it remains in effect. Most of the opposition to it is centered in organized minority groups who feel, with some justification, that both its quota system and its administration are stacked against the people and the areas where emigration is most needful and pressing. To this proponents of the act [e.g. Frank L. Auerbach, below] reply that immigration, both quota and nonquota, reached a normal peak in 1954 under the act, as did the number of nonimmigrant entries. They also point out that few of the quotas, even for those areas alleged to be discriminated against, are actually filled. And the opposition retorts that the rigid screening process, which Charles H. Seaver examines below in the opening section of "The Stranger At Our Gates" and which they consider one of the worst features of the law, makes the filling of quotas almost impossible.

And so the debate rages, as will be seen by a reading of the articles in this section, and it will continue to rage so long as a single American has a friend or a relative or a favored cause beyond our borders.

PRESIDENT TRUMAN'S VETO OF
THE McCARRAN-WALTER BILL [1]

I return herewith, without my approval, H.R.5678, the proposed Immigration and Nationality Act.

In outlining my objections to this bill, I want to make it clear that it contains certain provisions that meet with my approval. This is a long and complex piece of legislation. It has 164 separate sections, some with more than forty subdivisions. It presents a difficult problem of weighing the good against the bad, and arriving at a judgment on the whole.

H.R.5678 is an omnibus bill which would revise and codify all of our laws relating to immigration, naturalization, and nationality.

[1] Reprinted from *United States Department of State Bulletin.* 27:78-82. July 14, 1952.

A general revision and modernization of these laws unquestionably is needed and long overdue, particularly with respect to immigration. But this bill would not provide us with an immigration policy adequate for the present world situation. Indeed, the bill, taking all its provisions together, would be a step backward and not a step forward. In view of the crying need for reform in the field of immigration, I deeply regret that I am unable to approve H.R.5678.

In recent years, our immigration policy has become a matter of major national concern. Long dormant questions about the effect of our immigration laws now assume first rate importance. What we do in the field of immigration and naturalization is vital to the continued growth and internal development of the United States—to the economic and social strength of our country—which is the core of the defense of the free world. Our immigration policy is equally, if not more important to the conduct of our foreign relations and to our responsibilities of moral leadership in the struggle for world peace.

In one respect, this bill recognizes the great international significance of our immigration and naturalization policy, and takes a step to improve existing laws. All racial bars to naturalization would be removed, and at least some minimum immigration quota would be afforded to each of the free nations of Asia.

I have long urged that racial or national barriers to naturalization be abolished. This was one of the recommendations in my civil rights message to the Congress on February 2, 1948. On February 19, 1951, the House of Representatives unanimously passed a bill to carry it out.

But now this most desirable provision comes before me embedded in a mass of legislation which would perpetuate injustices of long standing against many other nations of the world, hamper the efforts we are making to rally the men of East and West alike to the cause of freedom, and intensify the repressive and inhumane aspects of our immigration procedures. The price is too high, and in good conscience I cannot agree to pay it.

I want all our residents of Japanese ancestry, and all our friends throughout the Far East, to understand this point clearly. I cannot take the step I would like to take, and strike down the bars that prejudice has erected against them, without, at the same time, establishing new discriminations against the peoples of Asia and approving harsh and repressive measures directed at all who seek a new life within our boundaries. I am sure that with a little more time and a little more discussion in this country the public conscience and the good sense of the American people will assert themselves and we shall be in a position to enact an immigration and naturalization policy that will be fair to all.

In addition to removing racial bars to naturalization, the bill would permit American women citizens to bring their alien husbands to this country as nonquota immigrants, and enable alien husbands of resident women aliens to come in under the quota in a preferred status. These provisions would be a step toward preserving the integrity of the family under our immigration laws, and are clearly desirable.

The bill would also relieve transportation companies of some of the unjustified burdens and penalties now imposed upon them. In particular, it would put an end to the archaic requirement that carriers pay the expenses of aliens detained at the port of entry, even though such aliens have arrived with proper travel documents.

But these few improvements are heavily outweighed by other provisions of the bill which retain existing defects in our laws, and add many undesirable new features.

The bill would continue, practically without change, the national origins quota system, which was enacted into law in 1924, and put into effect in 1929. This quota system—always based upon assumptions at variance with our American ideals—is long since out of date and more than ever unrealistic in the face of present world conditions.

This system hinders us in dealing with current immigration problems, and is a constant handicap in the conduct of our foreign relations. As I stated in my message to Congress on March 24, 1952, on the need for an emergency program of immigration from Europe, "Our present quota system is not only inadequate to meet present emergency needs, it is also an obstacle to the development of an enlightened and satisfactory immigration policy for the long-run future."

The inadequacy of the present quota system has been demonstrated since the end of the war, when we were compelled to resort to emergency legislation to admit displaced persons. If the quota system remains unchanged, we shall be compelled to resort to similar emergency legislation again, in order to admit any substantial portion of the refugees from communism or the victims of overcrowding in Europe.

With the idea of quotas in general there is no quarrel. Some numerical limitation must be set, so that immigration will be within our capacity to absorb. But the over-all limitation of numbers imposed by the national origins quota system is too small for our needs today, and the country by country limitations create a pattern that is insulting to large numbers of our finest citizens, irritating to our allies abroad, and foreign to our purposes and ideals.

The over-all quota limitation, under the law of 1924, restricted annual immigration to approximately 150,000. This was about one seventh of 1 per cent of our total population in 1920. Taking into account the growth in population since 1920, the law now allows us but one tenth of 1 per cent of our total population. And since the largest national quotas are only partly used, the number actually coming in has been in the neighborhood of one fifteenth of 1 per cent. This is far less than we must have in the years ahead to keep up with the growing needs of our nation for manpower to maintain the strength and vigor of our economy.

The greatest vice of the present quota system, however, is that it discriminates, deliberately and intentionally, against many of the peoples of the world. The purpose behind it was to cut down and virtually eliminate immigration to this country from Southern and Eastern Europe. A theory was invented to rationalize this objective. The theory was that in order to be readily assimilable, European immigrants should be admitted in proportion to the numbers of persons of their respective national stocks already here as shown by the census of 1920. Since Americans of English, Irish and German descent were most numerous, immigrants of those three nationalities got the lion's share—more than two thirds—of the total quota. The remaining third was divided up among all the other nations given quotas.

The desired effect was obtained. Immigration from the newer sources of Southern and Eastern Europe was reduced to a trickle. The quotas allotted to England and Ireland remained largely unused, as was intended. Total quota immigration fell to a half or a third—and sometimes even less—of the annual limit of 154,000. People from such countries as Greece, or Spain, or Latvia were virtually deprived of any opportunity to come here at all, simply because Greeks or Spaniards or Latvians had not come here before 1920 in any substantial numbers.

The idea behind this discriminatory policy was, to put it baldly, that Americans with English or Irish names were better people and better citizens than Americans with Italian or Greek or Polish names. It was thought that people of West European origin made better citizens than Rumanians or Yugoslavs or Ukrainians or Hungarians or Balts or Austrians. Such a concept is utterly unworthy of our traditions and our ideals. It violates the great political doctrine of the Declaration of Independence that "all men are created equal." It denies the humanitarian creed inscribed beneath the Statue of Liberty proclaiming to all nations, "Give me your tired, your poor, your huddled masses yearning to breathe free."

It repudiates our basic religious concepts, our belief in the brotherhood of man, and in the words of St. Paul that "there is neither Jew nor Greek, there is neither bond nor free, . . . for ye are all one in Christ Jesus."

The basis of this quota system was false and unworthy in 1924. It is even worse now. At the present time, this quota system keeps out the very people we want to bring in. It is incredible to me that, in this year of 1952, we should again be enacting into law such a slur on the patriotism, the capacity, and the decency of a large part of our citizenry.

Today, we have entered into an alliance, the North Atlantic Treaty, with Italy, Greece, and Turkey against one of the most terrible threats mankind has ever faced. We are asking them to join with us in protecting the peace of the world. We are helping them to build their defenses, and train their men, in the common cause. But, through this bill we say to their people: You are less worthy to come to this country than Englishmen or Irishmen; you Italians, who need to find homes abroad in the hundreds of thousands—you shall have a quota of 5,645; you Greeks, struggling to assist the helpless victims of a Communist civil war—you shall have a quota of 308; and you Turks, you are brave defenders of the Eastern flank, but you shall have a quota of only 225!

Today, we are "protecting" ourselves, as we were in 1924, against being flooded by immigrants from Eastern Europe. This is fantastic. The countries of Eastern Europe have fallen under the Communist yoke—they are silenced, fenced off by barbed wire and minefields—no one passes their borders but at the risk of his life. We do not need to be protected against immigrants from these countries—on the contrary we want to stretch out a helping hand, to save those who have managed to flee into Western Europe, to succor those who are brave enough to escape from barbarism, to welcome and restore them against the day when their countries will, as we hope, be free again. But this we cannot do, as we would like to do, because the quota for Poland is only 6,500, as against the 138,000 exiled Poles, all over Europe, who are asking to come to these shores; because the quota for the now subjugated Baltic countries is little more than 700— against the 23,000 Baltic refugees imploring us to admit them to a new life here; because the quota for Rumania is only 289, and some 30,000 Rumanians, who have managed to escape the labor camps and the mass deportations of their Soviet masters, have asked our help. These are only a few examples of the absurdity, the cruelty of carrying over into this year of 1952 the isolationist limitations of our 1924 law.

In no other realm of our national life are we so hampered and stultified by the dead hand of the past, as we are in this field of immigration. We do not limit our cities to their 1920 boundaries—we do not hold our corporations to their 1920 capitalizations—we welcome progress and change to meet changing conditions in every sphere of life, except in the field of immigration.

The time to shake off this dead weight of past mistakes is now. The time to develop a decent policy of immigration—a fitting instrument for our foreign policy and a true reflection of the ideals we stand for, at home and abroad—is now. . . .

I now wish to turn to the other provisions of the bill, those dealing with the qualifications of aliens and immigrants for admission, with the administration of the laws, and with problems of naturalization and nationality. In these provisions too, I find objections that preclude my signing this bill.

The bill would make it even more difficult to enter our country. Our resident aliens would be more easily separated from homes and families under grounds of deportation, both new and old, which would specifically be made retroactive. Admission to our citizenship would be made more difficult; expulsion from our citizenship would be made easier. Certain rights of native born, first generation Americans would be limited. All our citizens returning from abroad would be subjected to serious risk of unreasonable invasions of privacy. Seldom has a bill exhibited the distrust evidenced here for citizens and aliens alike—at a time when we need unity at home, and the confidence of our friends abroad.

We have adequate and fair provisions in our present law to protect us against the entry of criminals. The changes made by the bill in those provisions would result in empowering minor immigration and consular officials to act as prosecutor, judge and jury in determining whether acts constituting a crime have been committed. Worse, we would be compelled to exclude certain people because they have been convicted by "courts" in Communist countries that know no justice. Under this provision, no matter how construed, it would not be possible for us to admit many of the men and women who have stood up against totalitarian repression and have been punished for doing so. I do not approve of substituting totalitarian vengeance for democratic justice. I will not extend full faith and credit to the judgments of the Communist secret police.

The realities of a world, only partly free, would again be ignored in the provision flatly barring entry to those who have made misrepresentations in securing visas. To save their lives and the lives of loved ones still imprisoned, refugees from tyranny sometimes misstate various details of their lives. We do not want to encourage fraud. But we must recognize that conditions in some parts of the world drive our friends to desperate steps. An exception restricted to cases involving misstatement of country of birth is not sufficient. And to make refugees from oppression forever deportable on such technical grounds is shabby treatment indeed.

Some of the new grounds of deportation which the bill would provide are unnecessarily severe. Defects and mistakes in admission would serve to deport at any time because of the bill's elimination, retroactively as well as prospectively, of the present humane provision barring deportations on such grounds five years after entry. Narcotic drug addicts would be deportable at any time, whether or not the addiction was culpable, and whether or not cured. The threat of deportation would drive the addict into hiding beyond the reach of cure, and the danger to the country from drug addiction would be increased.

I am asked to approve the reenactment of highly objectionable provisions now contained in the Internal Security Act of 1950—a measure passed over my veto shortly after the invasion of South Korea. Some of these provisions would empower the Attorney General to deport any alien who has engaged or has had a purpose to engage in activities "prejudicial to the public interest" or "subversive to the national security." No standards or definitions are provided to guide discretion in the exercise of powers so sweeping. To punish undefined "activities" departs from traditional American insistence on established standards of guilt. To punish an undefined "purpose" is thought control.

These provisions are worse than the infamous Alien Act of 1798, passed in a time of national fear and distrust of foreigners, which gave the President power to deport any alien deemed "dangerous to the peace and safety of the United States." Alien residents were thoroughly frightened and citizens much disturbed by that threat to liberty.

Such powers are inconsistent with our democratic ideals. Conferring powers like that upon the Attorney General is unfair to him as well as to our alien residents. Once fully informed of such vast discretionary powers vested in the Attorney General, Americans now would and should be just as alarmed as Americans were in 1798 over less drastic powers vested in the President.

Heretofore, for the most part, deportation and exclusion have rested upon findings of fact made upon evidence. Under this bill, they would rest in many instances upon the "opinion" or "satisfaction" of immigration or consular employees. The change from objective findings to subjective feelings is not compatible with our system of justice. The result would be to restrict or eliminate judicial review of unlawful administrative action.

The bill would sharply restrict the present opportunity of citizens and alien residents to save family members from deportation. Under the procedures of present law, the Attorney General can exercise his discretion to suspend deportation in meritorious cases. In each such case, at the present time, the exercise of administrative discretion is subject to the scrutiny and approval of the Congress. Nevertheless, the bill would prevent this discretion from being used in many cases where it is now available, and would narrow the circle of those who can obtain relief from the letter of the law. This is most unfortunate, because the bill, in its other provisions, would impose harsher restrictions and greatly increase the number of cases deserving equitable relief.

Native-born American citizens who are dual nationals would be subjected to loss of citizenship on grounds not applicable to other native-born American citizens. This distinction is a slap at millions of Americans whose fathers were of alien birth.

Children would be subjected to additional risk of loss of citizenship. Naturalized citizens would be subjected to the risk of denaturalization by any procedure that can be found to be permitted under any state law or practice pertaining to minor civil law suits. Judicial review of administrative denials of citizenship would be severely limited and impeded in many cases, and completely eliminated in others. I believe these provisions raise serious constitutional questions. Constitutionality aside, I see no justification in national policy for their adoption. . . .

In these and many other respects, the bill raises basic questions as to our fundamental immigration and naturalization policy, and the laws and practices for putting that policy into effect.

Many of the aspects of the bill which have been most widely criticized in the public debate are reaffirmations or elaborations of existing statutes or administrative procedures. Time and again, examination discloses that the revisions of existing law that would be made by the bill are intended to solidify some restrictive practice of our immigration authorities, or to overrule or modify some ameliorative decision of the Supreme Court or other Federal courts. By and large, the changes that would be made by the bill do not depart from the basically restrictive spirit of our existing laws—but intensify and reinforce it.

These conclusions point to an underlying condition which deserves the most careful study. Should we not undertake a reassessment of our immigration policies and practices in the light of the conditions that face us in the second half of the twentieth century? The great popular interest which this bill has created, and the criticisms which it has stirred up, demand an affirmative answer. I hope the Congress will agree to a careful reexamination of this entire matter.

To assist in this complex task, I suggest the creation of a representative commission of outstanding Americans to examine the basic assumptions of our immigration policy, the quota system and all that goes with it, the effect of our present immigration and nationality laws, their administration, and the ways in which they can be brought into line with our national ideals and our foreign policy.

Such a commission should, I believe, be established by the Congress. Its membership should be bi-partisan and divided equally among persons from private life and persons from public life. I suggest that four members be appointed by the President, four by the President of the Senate, and four by the Speaker of the House of Representatives. The commission should be given sufficient funds to employ a staff and it should have adequate powers to hold hearings, take testimony, and obtain information. It should make a report to the President and to the Congress within a year from the time of its creation. [See "Time For A Change?" in Section IV, below.]

Pending the completion of studies by such a commission, and the consideration of its recommendations by the Congress, there are certain steps which I believe it is most important for the Congress to take this year.

First, I urge the Congress to enact legislation removing racial barriers against Asians from our laws. . . .

Second, I strongly urge the Congress to enact the temporary, emergency immigration legislation which I recommended three months ago . . . to authorize the admission of 300,000 additional immigrants to the United States over a three-year period. . . .

I very much hope that the Congress will take early action on these recommendations. Legislation to carry them out will correct some of the unjust provisions of our laws, will strengthen us at home and abroad, and will serve to relieve a great deal of the suffering and tension existing in the world today.

ON THE OTHER HAND [2]

Few domestic problems more directly involve the future of the United States than immigration. Few hotter issues face Congress and the Administration than the McCarran-Walter Act, which, last December, became our basic immigration law.

Why has this law been so bitterly attacked?

Some of the attack has been political—a result of the mistaken idea of some politicians that a bars-down immigration law is the way to win votes from so-called "minority groups" in this country. Some of the attack—the most vicious and violent part of it—has been led by Communist and left-wing organizations rightly fearful of its more rigid restraints on subversives. Not since the campaign to discredit Chiang Kai-shek and prepare the way for the Communist conquest of China have leftist forces in the United States been so aggressively united as in opposition to this law.

[2] From "The Truth About the Immigration Act," by Representative Francis E. Walter (Democrat, Pennsylvania), chairman of the House Un-American Committee in the Eighty-fourth Congress, and co-author, with the late Senator Pat McCarran of Nevada, of the Immigration and Nationality Act of 1952. *Reader's Digest.* 62: 126-32. May 1953. Reprinted by permission.

The campaign of misrepresentation which these forces have loosed is without parallel in recent legislative history. As a result, some newspapers, commentators and numerous organizations have been grossly misled into joining the opposition. Hearing and reading their wholly unjustified attacks on the law, I am sure of one thing: They have never read it.

What is the background of this law? Both of its authors are Democrats. The House and Senate subcommittees charged with the bill's preparation each had five Democrats and four Republicans. In both subcommittees the vote for the bill was unanimous.

For the bipartisan support which the measure finally won, much credit must go to the members of both House and Senate committees and particularly to Senator McCarran, who gave notable leadership in the preparation and passage of the Act.

The House vote on the bill was 206 for, 68 against. The favorable vote in the Senate was unrecorded.

President Truman vetoed the bill. Congress speedily overrode his veto by 278 to 113 in the House, 57 to 26 in the Senate.

Is it true, as charged, that the McCarran-Walter Act is "hysterical" legislation which was "rushed through Congress"?

The nearly five years of hearings, investigations and research which went into the preparation of this law are said to be the longest period ever devoted to a single piece of legislation in the history of Congress. Public testimony, for and against, was taken from nearly a thousand persons: experts, Government officials, representatives of all of the groups concerned with the problem.

The two Federal agencies directly responsible for administering immigration and naturalization laws—the Departments of State and Justice—both set up committees of experts which gave continuous aid to the joint committee.

This long process of preparation was due to the determination of Senator McCarran and myself and the members of our committees that our bill, insofar as humanly possible, should be sound and workable and for the best interests of our country. As a result, the Act—a document of three hundred pages—was put through six complete revisions. The resulting measure, for the first time in our history, clarifies and codifies all of our previous hundreds of immigration enactments into a single law.

The Departments of State and Justice both endorsed the bill as finally written. So did the Central Intelligence Agency. The head of the Immigration and Naturalization Service called it "a desirable revision of our immigration and naturalization laws." No Government agency opposed it. . . .

What is the truth about this law? Is it, as charged, "reactionary," "fascist," "racist"?

The facts are that, in important particulars, it is the most liberal immigration law in United States history.

For the first time, all racial bars to immigration are removed. Asiatic countries are given annual immigrant quotas determined by the same formula as quotas for Europe.

For the first time, all racial bars to naturalization are removed. Thus, 85,000 Orientals now living in the United States and Hawaii, heretofore ineligible for citizenship, may become citizens. . . .

For the first time, provision is made to permit the quota-free entrance of the alien wives, husbands and children of United States citizens. The national president of the YWCA testified before the Senate-House Committee: "We are delighted that the proposed revisions of the law are designed to further the preservation of family units."

For the first time, the doctrine "Once a Communist always a Communist" is rejected. A "redemptive" clause in the law makes eligible for entry ex-Communists who have proved a bona fide change of heart.

A spokesman for the American Civil Liberties Union said: "I want to express our agreement with the principle that past membership in either Communist or other totalitarian organizations will not forever be a bar to immigration into the United States."

Is it true, as charged, that the Immigration Act introduces "new forms of racial discrimination" which make it "an insult to all Asia"?

On the contrary, Asia, for the first time, is on a basis of equality. Special provision, however, had to be made for Asiatics residing outside Asia. There are 600,000 persons of Asiatic descent living in Central and South America, in countries for which there is no numerical limitation for immigration. Brazil recently entered into an agreement with Japan to admit fifty thousand Japanese nationals. To maintain the fairness of the quota system, the law now provides that such persons must enter the United States under the quota of the country of their racial origin.

This restriction was prepared with the active assistance of representatives of organizations of Asiatics in the United States. Every such important organization has gone on record endorsing the McCarran-Walter Act.

Is it true, as charged, that the new law "reduces the flow of immigrants to a trickle"?

With more generous provision for certain nonquota groups, and with quotas granted, for the first time, to eleven Asiatic countries, the total annual immigration to the United States is increased by a possible 25 per cent—from 155,000 to approximately 200,000.

Is it true, as charged, that the Immigration Act "narrows the gateway to the United States" by requiring that 50 per cent of immigrants "must be persons of high education, specialized experience or exceptional ability"?

The law ends the old policy of accepting immigrants on the basis of "first come, first served." It establishes a policy of selectivity—similar to that of every other immigrant-receiving nation—aimed to secure those immigrants most likely to fit usefully into our economy and culture. To that end it sets up three categories of immigrants: persons of skilled or exceptional training; relatives of American citizens; other immigrants.

Fifty per cent of each quota is reserved for the first—the skilled—category. The choice, here, is made as a result of specific requests by United States employers to the Attorney General. If, for example, dyemakers are in short supply, companies needing such skilled labor appeal to the Department of Justice, which, through the United States Employment Service, verifies the need and instructs our overseas representatives to give preferred status to such workers.

The law, however, does not prescribe that 50 per cent must be from that first category. If there are fewer than 50 per cent of such persons on the list, then the quota is filled, as far as possible, from the second category. After those categories have been cleared, the remaining number are automatically assigned to the third category.

Is it true, as charged, that the new law "blunts one of our most important psychological weapons in the cold war" by preventing most of the people who escape from behind the Iron Curtain from reaching their hoped-for refuge in the United States?

Of the more than one million European refugees resettled by the International Refugee Organization, one out of three has been taken by the United States. Yet today, in West Germany alone, there are ten million refugees from communism. In other free areas of Europe there are probably that many more.

"It is demagogy to contend," says the Washington *News,* "that this country can become a sanctuary for 'most' of these people. To lower our immigration bars will not solve this problem but only create a problem of our own."

Should our immigration policy, as proposed by the Truman commission, [President Truman's Commission on Immigration and Naturalization; see "Time For A Change?" in Section IV, below] be "flexible enough to relieve overpopulation" and "permit the United States to engage fully in such migration efforts as may be important to the security of the free world"?

In Europe alone overpopulation has been estimated as high as 79 million. Yet every year Europe's population increases by another three million. A present proposal aims to move out five million people in the next ten years—not noticeably affecting the problem.

"The United States," says the New York *World-Telegram,* "should do all it can to assist these people in finding new homes in areas of opportunity. But this country has long since passed the point where it can operate under a policy of unrestricted immigration, which is virtually what some people are seeking."

Last year I was a United States delegate to the meeting in Brussels which set up a 26-nation Organization for the Movement of Refugees from Europe. Our Government, I am proud to say, is taking the lead in attacking that problem. We must continue and increase our support for that work.

We must also, if the need arises, meet special problems with emergency legislation—as we have done during and since the war. But such special and emergency provisions should not be a part of our basic immigration law.

Is it true, as charged, that the new law "makes easy the deportation of thousands of worthy people"; that "it makes denaturalization a daily possibility for naturalized citizens"?

The Immigration Act excludes from the United States any alien whose presence would endanger the public safety. It provides for the deportation of any alien who engages in activities endangering the public safety.

Back of these provisions is a problem of serious proportions. At present there are from three million to five million aliens illegally in the United States. Deportation orders had already been issued for thousands of these persons. But, because of loopholes in the old law, these orders were unenforceable. As a result, thousands of criminals and subversive aliens are roaming our streets, a continuing threat to the safety of our country.

Another equally startling fact: The then United States Attorney General presented to our committee an analysis of approximately five thousand "of the more militant members of the Communist Party." This analysis showed that 91.5 per cent of them were either of foreign birth, married to persons of foreign birth or born of foreign parents, and that over half of them traced their origins either to Russia or to her satellite countries.

With these and other facts before us, we wrote a law which makes it tougher for aliens to get into this country illegally. It makes it a crime for them to conceal their illegal status. It sets up better machinery for deporting them. It provides that naturalized citizens can be denaturalized and deported if, within five years of their naturalization, they join in subversive activity.

But the new law also provides that in every deportation case a hearing is mandatory and appeal to the courts is permitted. It also provides that in every case involving the revocation of citizenship the courts—and only the courts—can make the decision. In addition to this procedure the writ of habeas corpus is available.

Frank L. Auerbach, immigration expert in the Department of State, says: "The procedural safeguards afforded by the new act to an alien subject to deportation are greater than those enjoyed under the old law."

Aiming for a laxer law, the enemies of the Immigration Act center their heaviest attack on the national-origins quota system —the basis of our present policy. That system, said Mr. Truman, "breathes prejudice against the foreign-born." To the Truman commission it is "racial and religious discrimination."

The national-origins quota system has been basic to our immigration policy since 1924. Under it the United States has admitted, since 1929, nearly five million immigrants.

Through the use of an established, uniform formula or rule of law, that system is designed to do four things:

To limit the annual number of quota immigrants who can come to the United States;

To determine the nationality of those who come so as to maintain the historic population pattern of the United States;

To put all quota nations on an equal footing;

To keep the immigration problem beyond the reach of politics and pressure groups.

By the national-origins formula, the number of quota immigrants from each country is limited to one sixth of 1 per cent of the inhabitants of the United States who in 1920 traced their origins to that particular country. That works out to an annual total, from 85 countries, of 154,657 immigrants—exclusive of nonquota immigrants.

By this system the number from each country is determined by mathematicians, not politicians. . . .

The defense of this system has been well put by the *Christian Science Monitor*:

> We believe it is a mistake to condemn any quota system based on national origins as inherently illiberal and an expression of religious or racial prejudice. It is no reflection on the many fine American citizens of all races, creeds and national origins to recognize realistically that some nations are far closer to the United States in culture, custom and standard of living, respect for law and experience in self-government.

What is the alternative proposed by the Truman commission?

Instead of a national-origins quota system it proposes "a unified quota system."

That system would provide no uniform, nonpolitical means for determining the source of immigration. It would vest in "an administrative agency" appointed by the President the vast power of choosing among nationalities.

Thus, this highly explosive problem would be brought within easy reach of politics and special-interest pressures. Instead of the present system under which "quotas are definite and automatically resist the pressure of special groups," says the New York *Herald Tribune,* we would have a system where "quotas are indefinite and automatically invite such pressures."

Is it not true that some countries, most notably Great Britain, do not use up their annual quotas and would it not be a good policy to distribute those unused quota numbers, at the end of every year, to nations where more people desire to come than, on their quotas, are permitted?

Our joint committee of seven senators and seven representatives gave this problem serious study over many months. The question before us was simply this: By what means, free from political pressures, could these unused quotas be distributed?

To this question we were given two answers. The first was: Give the numbers to the nation where there was the greatest pressure to come. That country, we found, was China. The second answer was: Distribute the unused quotas on a basis of first come, first served. That proposal, we concluded, was administratively impossible to carry out and, even worse, it opened the door wide to the exercise of all kinds of political and group pressures and consequent ill will, both here and abroad.

The present law will undoubtedly undergo minor revisions as experience with its operation dictates. There have been some cases of individual hardship in its early application. Some of these cases have aroused what I believe will prove to be unjustified apprehensions among some of our friends abroad. I regret this and I am sure that, as the administration of the law improves, these incidents will not recur.

The aim of the opponents of this law is not to better its execution or revise its provisions but to destroy it. The issue thereby raised is clear. Are we to have an immigration policy—impossible of fulfillment—based primarily on the desires of Europe? Or are we to have a policy which is based primarily on what is good for America?

THE STRANGER AT OUR GATES [3]

The first step toward immigration to the United States is to apply for a visa at a consular office or consular section of an embassy or other "diplomatic mission." In 1952 there were 263 such posts in foreign countries where visas are issued, of which 48 have one or more officers assigned to this work for full time. A visa is practically a permit to apply for admission at some port of entry (land "port" or seaport). Each applicant for a visa must prepare a long application, with whatever documentary evidence he can show to verify his statements (refugees and escapees are likely to have few documents). Then he is examined under oath concerning his background, opinions, and intentions. At the same time other sources of information are used if available and practicable. An unfavorable report from any source is likely to end the proceedings.

There are forty to fifty items and about five thousand words in the section (212) of the present Immigration and Nationality

[3] From *As We Do Unto Others*, booklet by Charles H. Seaver, writer and editorial consultant for the Department of International Justice and Goodwill, National Council of the Churches of Christ in the U.S.A. The Department. 120 East 23d Street. New York 10. 1952. p 13-21. Permission to reprint is granted by Charles H. Seaver, who originally wrote this material for the Department of International Justice and Goodwill of the National Council of the Churches of Christ in the U.S.A. Responsibility for the material in the booklet is solely that of the author.

Act citing causes for refusal of visas to applicants or refusal of admission as immigrants. The most controversial items are those intended to screen out present or potential "subversives." These run to about 1,500 words. Most of the causes stated are reasonably clear and appropriate, but a few are questionable.

One example cited by opponents of the Act is that a person who has ever been a member of a party or group advocating Communist doctrines be denied a visa unless this membership was "involuntary" or he has been for at least five years "actively opposed to its doctrine, program, principles, and ideology." The very reason many persons have fled from their native countries to seek new homes elsewhere is that outward conformity to the existing regime was essential to safety and "active opposition" would have been quickly suppressed. The ban against former followers of other totalitarian doctrines, however, such as nazism, Italian fascism, and Spanish falangism, though included in an earlier law and in an earlier draft of this Act, was for some reason removed from the final draft.

The consular officer also is expected to exercise his personal judgment whether or not the admission of each particular applicant would be "in the public interest." If his opinion is negative, that is usually final, since few applicants have means or facilities for appeal. If the consular officer believes the applicant "would, after entry, engage in any activity the purpose of which is opposition to the government of the United States," the applicant is ineligible. This provision is capable of varying interpretation, according to the prejudices or imagination of the consular officer—or according to the attitude of his superiors in the consulate or in Washington toward immigration. The consular officer is required also to refuse visas to any aliens who in his opinion "are likely at any time to become public charges" —which involves a rare degree of foresight. What applicant could prove that he would never become a public charge?

Another controversial provision is that persons are ineligible to receive visas "who have been convicted of two or more offenses (other than political offenses)," regardless of "whether the conviction was in a single trial, or the offenses arose from a single scheme of misconduct, or the offenses involved moral turpitude, for which the aggregate sentences to confinement actually imposed were five years or more." Another clause excludes "aliens who have been convicted of a crime involving moral turpitude (other than a purely political offense) or aliens who admit having committed such a crime." It is well known that convictions of political opponents or suspected nonconformists or of prisoners in concentration camps have often been obtained in totalitarian countries on trumped-up charges of nonpolitical offenses (including "moral turpitude," however that term may be interpreted). Critics of these provisions, therefore, suggest requiring more than the judgment of a minor official in such cases; they object to substituting totalitarian for American standards of justice.

On the same grounds, immigrants with visas may be excluded on arrival at ports of entry. Visas are issued by consular officers of the Department of State; immigrants are screened on arrival by agents of Immigration and Naturalization Service, which is a division of the Department of Justice. Their decisions are not bound by those of consular officers abroad. An applicant having a valid visa may thus be refused entry. The Attorney General is the final arbiter of cases arising under the Act (but this means, in practice, some subordinate official), except as Congress may pass special laws admitting certain immigrants. (Over two thousand such bills were introduced in the Eighty-second Congress, and over 700 passed, affecting about 1,400 persons).

The Hoover Commission [on Reorganization of the United States Executive Departments] recommended that all authority over immigration, including the issuance of visas, be centered in one agency, so that when an applicant receives a visa he will be assured of admission, except for intervening causes. It proposed that this agency be the Department of Justice. The President's Commission, reflecting opinion that the Department of Justice, as a litigating and prosecuting agency, was unsuitable for this administrative function, recommended that an independent agency be set up to have charge of all immigration (and naturalization) functions. . . .

Many supporters of the law, however, are inclined to follow the lead of some in denouncing critics of the present screening process as "reds," "pinks," "liberals," and "demagogues who would auction the interest of America for alleged minority-bloc votes." In the record of hearings before the President's Commission most of the opposition to any change reflects the attitude that the added barriers are needed to keep out "a flood of subversives." . . . It was even suggested that many "refugees" might have been delegated by Communist governments to emigrate to the United States. This seems to assume that subversive agents usually enter among regular immigrants and may be detected by the papers they carry or beliefs they profess, if the immigration law includes enough restrictions. . . .

Our Resident Aliens

There are about 2.5 million aliens resident in the United States. They are mainly immigrants who have been admitted for permanent residence but have not yet been naturalized; but there are also persons whose business or profession brings them here for extended stay but who do not wish to give up their foreign citizenship; persons accredited as representatives of foreign countries recognized by the United States or of a recognized international organization, including their families, employees, and attendants; and certain other special classes.

Except the group of foreign official representatives, every immigrant and nonimmigrant alien (eighteen years of age and over) admitted to the United States, after being registered and fingerprinted, must "at all times carry with him and have in his personal possession" his certificate or receipt showing registration. Otherwise he is subject to fine and imprisonment. He is required also to notify the Attorney General in writing of any change of address within ten days of such change. Failure to send such notice may be punished by deportation. (These provisions apply also to aliens admitted before such requirements were imposed.) If the alien is only a temporary resident, he must notify the Attorney General of his address at the expiration of each three-months' period, whether changed or not. Any employee of the Immigration Service has power without warrant, and at any time, "to interrogate any alien or person believed to be an alien as to his right to be or remain in the United States."

If it is discovered at any time that a resident alien was not eligible to entry for any reason at the time of entry—which may have been five, ten, or twenty or more years ago—he may be deported, even though he has lived here without serious transgression. If within five years of entry he has become a "public charge" by reason of illness or destitution, he is deportable unless he can prove that his condition did not result from causes existing prior to entry.

Under the old law an alien threatened with deportation could apply to the Attorney General to suspend deportation proceedings. The Attorney General could suspend such proceedings if in his opinion deportation would result in a "serious economic detriment" to members of his family. Under the present law the Attorney General may so act only in cases of "exceptional and extremely unusual hardship to the alien or his spouse, parents, or child," and then only if the alien "has been physically present in the United States for a continuous period of not less than seven years immediately preceding the date of such application, and proves that during all of such period he was and is a person of good moral character." If this alien had gone abroad for a few weeks during that period to visit relatives or dispose of some property, or even had spent a week with friends or relatives in Canada, the Attorney General apparently could do nothing for him. The letter of the law, however, is not always thus invoked.

It is risky otherwise also for an alien resident to leave the country, even if he has applied to the Attorney General for a re-entry permit, after stating his reasons for the trip. The permit merely identifies him. He must undergo examination again.

Those are cited as a few of the many examples of "tightening" the law as to resident aliens. A good deal of research would be required to determine whether each new "tighter" provision of this sort was prompted by evidence of an actual case or cases where it would have served a useful purpose, or was based on expectation of cases that might arise, or both. Advocates of these provisions would doubtless argue that hardships imposed on a few or even many innocuous resident aliens and their families would be justified if the same procedure resulted in the deportation of some actual or potential "subversives." Yet deportation (i.e., banishment) is a severe penalty for minor errors or offenses. American residents in England, France, Canada, or any other "free" country are not deportable for comparatively trivial reasons.

Without judgment as to the necessity or appropriateness of any particular "tightened" restriction, a thoughtful reader of the many pages and thousands of words used to set forth the conditions under which alien residents may keep or lose their residence can hardly avoid serious misgivings. He would sense in the law a strong suspicion of alien residents in general and a determination to make their presence among us increasingly uncomfortable. One is reminded of the displays used in anti-American demonstrations by Communists in some foreign countries, bearing in one or another language the words, "Americans, go home!" On the other hand, liberal and humane interpretation and administration of these provisions of the Act, with opportunity for appeal, might reduce injustices to a minimum. . . .

Our Naturalized Citizens

Some of our alien residents, of course, have come here with no expectation of becoming American citizens. They may not wish to give up their ties with their native lands, to which they expect to return for their old age, or when their earnings permit, or when the business or professional assignment that brought them is completed. Likewise many of our citizens become residents of other countries for short or long periods without giving up their American citizenship. Alien status in a country is not, or should not be, nor has it been in the United States in earlier years, a bar to creative contributions.

But most of the aliens admitted to the United States as immigrants seek American citizenship sooner or later. About 7.5 million of our present citizens are citizens by naturalization rather than by birth; still more are children of such citizens. An alien admitted for permanent residence may declare, at any time, his intention to become a citizen; but may not apply for his final citizenship papers until he has resided in the United States for five years, and in the state for at least six months. There are some exceptions to this requirement, as wives or husbands of citizens and veterans, who may apply on shorter residence. Other requirements are age of eighteen or over, ability to read and write English, "a knowledge and understanding of the fundamentals of the history and of the principles and form of government of the United States," and "a good moral character, attached to the principles of the Constitution and well disposed to the good order and happiness of the United States." Children born in the United States are citizens; also children born outside if the parents are citizens, or when they become citizens; and naturalization of the parents, or a surviving parent, gives children under sixteen American citizenship. The recent legislation has added many details intended to deny citizenship to applicants suspected of Communist opinions, membership in a Communist organization, or association with Communists.

The Act of 1952, however, made also some significant improvements in the naturalization laws. (1) It abolished remaining racial disqualifications, so that residents of Oriental birth may now become citizens by the same process as those of European birth. (2) It confirmed the right of naturalization to conscientious objectors to armed service (on religious grounds). (3) It removed the need of a prior declaration of intention. (4) It exempted older persons from the literacy requirement. At the same time it requires personal investigation of every applicant's conduct for the preceding five years to determine "moral character," etc., and takes from the courts their one-time discretion in this regard, by elaborating in great detail the indications of immoral or unmoral character. And a long list of "subversive" indications is added as barriers to naturalization.

A very controversial feature of the Immigration and Naturalization Act, however, is its creation of a "second-class" citizenship. Citizenship once granted by the regular judicial process was formerly supposed to be full citizenship—the same as that of native-born citizens—unless it could be shown that it was obtained by fraud or other illegality. The Constitution makes no distinction between native and naturalized citizens as to their rights. Chief Justice Marshall's famous statement about the naturalized citizen may well be cited: that he becomes "a member of the society, possessing all the rights of a native citizen and standing, in the view of the Constitution, on the footing of a native." And he added: "The Constitution does not authorize Congress to enlarge or abridge those rights." But under the present Act many naturalized citizens live under continuous danger of denaturalization and deportation, even though their naturalization was obtained legally and without any misrepresentations.

It may be dangerous for a naturalized citizen to enter into any political activities or join any group or organization which may seek change—of labor or housing conditions, or local government, or any existing legislation. Communists also, unknown to the naturalized citizen, may be participating in the activity or be members of the group. The penalty may be loss of citizenship or deportation. It is reported that many naturalized citizens now are fearful of membership in any community organization or labor union. While under present administration of the law this fear may not be justified, their second-class status is incorporated in the law—usable unjustly whenever the anti-foreign tide rises higher. Another offense leading to loss of citizenship is "contempt of Congress," which may be resentment of the insinuation, insults, or abusive tactics of a single inquisitor. If there is reason for punishing these offenses, should severer penalties be enforced on naturalized than on native-born citizens? If the number of cases of injustices to citizens having this second-class status has been comparatively small, they are nevertheless likely to be widely publicized, especially among the people of the nationality group involved and also abroad.

Our Alien Visitors

Normally people travel with a good deal of freedom, in peacetime, to and through other countries than their own—for sight-seeing, visits to relatives or friends, participation in international conferences, lecture tours, etc. Before World War II few governments imposed serious obstacles to such travel. Then, following the War, Soviet Russia lowered the "Iron Curtain." Its satellites, including Communist China, followed this pattern. Some deviations from the pattern were permitted, but relatively few. In 1950 the (McCarran) Internal Security Act (now incorporated in the 1952 Immigration and Naturalization Act), while not lowering any "Iron Curtain," put up some embarrassing barriers here to normal unofficial international intercourse.

A "security clearance," substantially like what is required of immigrants, is now required of temporary visitors. Applicants for temporary visas include students, teachers, scholars, writers, lawyers, musicians, businessmen, engineers, and tourists. Some may wish merely to pass through the country; some may have been invited to address a religious or educational gathering or a meeting of scientists, or to meet a professional group for consultation, or to lecture at some university or college. Even if the admission of such a person is eventually found not dangerous to the national security, the applicant may be subjected to annoyances, embarrassment, or long delay. (Indeed the visa may not be issued until the occasion for the visit has passed.) Canada, Great Britain, France, Italy, and various other countries are therefore more suitable places for unofficial conferences where foreign participation is desired.

It may seem to many of us unwise to admit for public speaking or participation in unofficial international conferences any person who may have been or might be critical of any aspect of the "American way" of life. More than a hundred years ago Charles Dickens was allowed to travel around the country freely, though he aroused some patriotic indignation by writing a book critical of some American customs. Nevertheless he came again, many years later, for a series of readings; the door was open to both immigrants and visitors. The eminent author, who had meanwhile written acceptable books critical also of English laws and customs, was given a good reception. (There is no record that his lodgings or lecture halls were even picketed). As to "ideologies," many were current in America, and their promotion was usually tolerated in the middle years of the nineteenth century. The New York *Tribune* invited Karl Marx, who had been expelled from Germany, to write a series of letters explaining his social and economic views; and these were published with apparently no enduring influence upon the development of a quite different system.

Our forefathers could be quite narrow-minded in some ways, but, like the men of Athens, were disposed to lend an ear to whoever had anything to say. So we have inherited a culture that naturally drew largely from foreign "isms" in its early development, and has continued of course to be influenced by other cultures. We find that this composite "American way," while not perfect and ever changing, has been and is productive of increasing welfare and opportunity for our people. The erection of barriers to intercourse, official and unofficial, with the rest of the world has never been a part of that way. Nor is it likely to promote good will and friendship with our neighbors.

A related cause of international unpleasantness is found in the provisions of this Act regarding alien crewmen. The major maritime countries of the world in number of seagoing merchant vessels, next to the United States, are Great Britain, Norway, Sweden, and France. Thousands of foreign merchant ships enter our ports every year. Many of their crewmen wish to land temporarily during the stay of their vessel or while awaiting assignment to another—just as crewmen on American ships like to go ashore in foreign ports. Under the present Act, for the first time, alien crewmen cannot land "until they have been cross-examined concerning every detail of their past lives and political beliefs and association," as one senator has put it. They must fulfill the same requirements as immigrants seeking permanent residence. It is easy to appreciate the feeling of the seamen—and their countrymen here and at home. . . .

Our Dilemma

Altogether such obstacles erected against even a limited immigration, such treatment of alien residents and visitors, and such discrimination against naturalized citizens—beyond the practice of other free nations—are held to be not only unneighborly but also inconsistent with a foreign policy that seeks friends and allies in defense of freedom.

On the other side, it is argued that any substitute for this Act would be likely to weaken our defenses against subversion from within, and any breach in it by amendment would invite other breaches until the doors would be opened wide to undesirable and unassimilable immigrants—also to Communist infiltration. . . .

Of course there are also confirmed "nativist" groups who deplore the coming of so many "delayed Pilgrims" during the past fifty (or maybe one hundred) years and feel strongly that the "old stock" has been already too much diluted. They may be disturbed about alien penetration into our religious, social, or political life. In so far as the present law checks such penetration, they like it.

It is held also that it is for us alone, regardless of foreign opinion, to frame our legislation on such a vital matter as whom we shall admit as immigrants or alien residents or visitors, or what requirements we shall make of naturalized citizens. We do not attempt to interfere with other nations' legislation on these matters; so our decisions should not be determined by their possible impact outside.

It is true also that some who acknowledge the defects in the present Act, and are concerned about its effect on our national unity and our foreign policy, are fearful also of the emotional reaction to a conflict over amendment or repeal at this time. They recognize the spread of isolationism and authoritarianism, as politically powerful forces are eager to enforce conformity to their interpretations of "Americanism," regardless of civil rights. So, many who are aware of injustices and dangers in the Act, and want to remove them, would rather wait until this wave of manufactured emotion has subsided, and hesitate to take a definite stand.

AMERICA'S NEW FRONT-DOOR POLICY [4]

Present American immigration policy, it has been charged, embitters our friends, encourages our enemies and brings the good name of our country into disrepute. Such wholesale indictment is, I believe, unjustified. I should like to answer it.

The new law is a complete rewriting, the first in thirty years, of our vast and complex immigration procedures. It has been in effect . . . [since December 24, 1952]. No doubt its administration, in this early period, has been sometimes faulty, on occasion unnecessarily harsh. But time and experience are smoothing out the rough spots. And time and experience are pointing the way to some adjustments in the law itself.

Meanwhile, the total record, as distinguished from the exceptions, indicates that our immigration policy is still in the generous American tradition. Our treatment of desirable aliens, whether visitors or immigrants, is, in fact, fairer and more friendly today than at any other time in my experience.

Let me first point out that admission to the United States is not a right but a privilege, extended by our Government on certain conditions. Those conditions, laid down in the law, are aimed to safeguard our country against "undesirables"—the criminal, the subversive, the diseased—and to promote what the Congress believes to be our country's best interests.

Unlike many countries, where tourism is a major industry and where "undesirables" seeking admission are not a major problem, the United States does not write its immigration laws to attract millions of foreign visitors. We aim, rather, to give maximum protection to our own self-interest, while accepting responsibility in the world community. . . .

Since the end of the war the United States has extended welcome to more than 400,000 displaced persons, more than one third the total received by all the other countries of the world.

[4] From an article by Hervé J. L'Heureux, former chief of the Visa Division of the State Department and currently Supervising Consul General for Western Germany. *Reader's Digest.* 65:61-6. August 1954. Reprinted by permission.

And we have done more. For the million refugees who have been resettled in other lands, the United States has paid one third of the total transportation cost. Also, it was an American proposal which led, two years ago, to setting up the Intergovernmental Committee for European Migration, aimed to relieve Europe's overpopulation problem. Twenty-four nations are members. (The United States pays more than all the others combined.)

Now the doors to this country are being opened even more widely. Under an act passed last summer [the Refugee Relief Act of 1953] we shall receive in the next two years, over and above quota immigration, 209,000 additional refugees. To select and transport them we shall spent an estimated $50 million.

"This legislation," said President Eisenhower, "demonstrates again America's traditional concern for the homeless, the persecuted, the less fortunate of other lands." Here is an answer to those who charge that our immigration policy is one of unconcern for the world's needy.

Look, now, at . . . our treatment of visitors from other countries.

The number of visitors is constantly increasing. Here, as a significant sample, is the way we treat one large, important group of them.

This year there are more than 34,000 visiting students in the United States. That is the largest number on record. It is more than in any other country.

These students, from 127 countries, were admitted without distinction as to religion, nationality or race. About one third are Asians. With few exceptions, every student was personally met at the port of entry (generally by a representative of the voluntary Committee on Friendly Relations Among Foreign Students), sped through port inspections, given literature about the United States and started toward a school or college.

For more than five hundred of these student visitors, all expenses (round-trip travel, tuition, living costs) are being paid by the United States Government. Another 8500 get scholarship help from American schools where they are enrolled. For those obliged to earn part of their way, a clause of the new immigration law provides that, on recommendation of the school, permission for employment will be granted. As a result, more than five thousand have part-time work.

Under previous law, foreign students were limited in attendance to certain "accredited" institutions. This closed the door to many who sought practical, rather than academic, training. Under the new law, vocational, trade and business schools are now approved.

How our consular and immigration officials, in their administration of the law, contribute to this American welcome is attested by the head of the Committee on Friendly Relations: "From the time of his application for a United States visa to his final departure from the country, today's visiting student is met with more understanding and friendliness from American officials than at any time in my experience. . . .

Within the necessary conditions laid down in the law, our present policy also increases the convenience with which a foreigner can visit the United States on business or pleasure or en route to another country. Despite the magnitude of our security problem, it takes only about four weeks to obtain a visitor's or a transit visa in Western European countries. For the convenience of the traveler who has too little time to get a transit visa, the new law permits passage through the United States without any United States documents whatever.

This measure, more liberal than any previous law, was included at the strong urging of the airlines seeking more "in transit" business. Such a "document waiver" is issued by the airline without Government supervision. The visitor signs a card of identification, declares his intention to "make immediate and continuous transit" and agrees while in the United States to accept "close supervision."

Complaints, now diminishing, about this supervision are best answered by the fact that last year twenty thousand foreign travelers took advantage of the no-document privilege. This year the number is expected to be at least one third greater.

Experience over many years clearly shows that, under any immigration law, however carefully drawn, exceptional cases arise which on humanitarian grounds or in the public interest merit special consideration and action. Present policy gives considerable leeway to consular and immigration officers to deal with such cases.

Recently an Englishman, convicted ten years before of larceny, applied for a visa to visit his brother, who was seriously ill in New York. A strict interpretation of the law would have barred him. But, after inquiry, the American consul issued the visa. A Cuban who recently applied with his wife and son for immigrant visas might have been excluded because of his son's physical disability. But the consul, convinced the boy would not become a public charge, issued visas of permanent residence for the entire family. Early last year a Chicago chemical concern inquired about bringing in a famous Greek chemist to direct a new development project. The normal immigration quota for Greece was filled for four years in advance. Under the preference given in the new law to needed specialists, however, a visa for the chemist was speedily secured.

Last September a French radio writer, a one-time member of the French Communist party, applied in Paris for a visitor's visa. Under our previous immigration policy he would have been barred by the "once a Communist always a Communist" provision. The new law contains a "redemption clause" which permits former Communists who have broken with the party to enter the country. Under this provision the French writer, like numerous other one-time Communists, was admitted.

It is true that the security provisions of the new immigration laws are tighter than ever—reflecting the fact that our security problem is more serious. But it is also true that the present law goes further than any previous legislation to accord the alien the constitutional rights that are granted to American citizens.

In deportation proceedings, for example, it is provided that the alien must be given reasonable notice of the charges against him, that he may examine the evidence, present evidence in his own behalf, cross-examine Government witnesses and be represented by counsel of his own choosing.

Today more than 1,300 private immigration bills are pending before the Immigration Subcommittee of the United States Senate. Most of these bills are bona fide efforts to grant the right of permanent residence to especially deserving aliens who are not technically eligible under the law. Thus the massive machinery of our national government—from Committee report to congressional vote to presidential signature—is put into operation for the sole benefit of the individual noncitizen.

In another important area, that of naturalization, our treatment of foreigners meets the test of American fairness and generosity.

In San Francisco one day last summer, the courtroom of Federal judge Louis E. Goodman was the scene of an affecting drama. Standing solemnly in rows before the bench were 182 Japanese aliens. All of them had lived for years in the United States, had established homes, raised their families here. But they had been barred from citizenship by the Oriental exclusion clause in our former immigration law.

In 1952 the McCarran-Walter Immigration and Nationality Act wiped out the racial clause, eliminated such bars to immigration and naturalization. When, under that law, these Japanese applied for citizenship, they got immediate aid. From the Citizenship Division of the United States Immigration and Naturalization Service they received free textbooks and home-study courses. Free citizenship classes were open to them in California's public schools. Then came the big day.

After Judge Goodman had administered the oath and declared them citizens, Kay Kunisaha Mineta, a San Jose shoe salesman, stepped forward and spoke for the group: "Today our dream comes true. With the passing of the years, some stormy, some uncertain, we kept an abiding faith in the country of our choice. . . ."

For foreigners of all categories who seek to become citizens, there are nearly 3,500 citizenship classes operating in all our states, Hawaii and Alaska. More than fifteen thousand are enrolled in home-study courses. Last year the Immigration and Naturalization Service distributed 150,000 free textbooks for candidates.

Responsibility for proper enforcement of our immigration and naturalization laws rests primarily upon our consular officers abroad and the Immigration and Naturalization Service in the United States. At home and abroad, there are fewer than two thousand officials directly engaged in this vast job. While enforcing our laws and protecting our interests, they must hear complaints, adjust disputes and serve, on behalf of all Americans, as ambassadors of good will.

When one views the size and complexity of their task, the clamorous, often powerful pressures to which they are subjected, one wonders how they err so seldom; how, so generally, they do their duty by America's laws in a way that is a credit to America.

As an American, familiar with our past and present immigration policy, I am proud of our record.

McCARRAN-WALTER STIMULATES IMMIGRATION [5]

The Immigration and Nationality Act became law on June 27, 1952. It is fitting, therefore, that we review immigration to the United States and the effect the new law has had on its volume and make-up in the past three years. In speaking of immigration I should like to apply this term in its broader sense to include not only the movement of those who are coming to our shores to remain but also the flow of visitors and other nonimmigrants who return to their countries after the purpose of their visit has been completed.

If we first examine immigration in its narrower sense, which includes the movement of those who come to stay, we see that during the last decade the volume of immigration has risen from a low of 38,000 in 1945 to more than 208,000 in 1954. Only twice during this ten-year period did the number of immigrants exceed that of the year 1954. This was in 1950 and 1952 when special legislation authorized the issuance of visas chargeable to future quota years.

The flow of nonimmigrants to the United States has also continuously increased during the last decade. The high point for

[5] From "Immigration Today" by Frank L. Auerbach, special assistant to the Director, Visa Office, Department of State. *I & N Reporter* [*Immigration & Naturalization Reporter*]. 4:6-9. July 1955. Reprinted by permission.

this period was reached in 1954 when the Immigration and Naturalization Service counted more than 59 million entries of non-immigrants, including those of agricultural laborers, seamen and Canadian and Mexican border crossers. . . .

During the last decade the volume of quota immigration climbed from a low of 11,623 in 1945 to 94,098 in 1954. The 1954 volume of quota immigration was exceeded markedly by that of the four-year period from 1949 through 1952 when 661,300 quota immigrants entered the United States. This peak in quota immigration during the years 1949 through 1952 was due to the provision of the Displaced Persons Act of 1948 which required that visas issued under it, except those to orphans, be charged to future quota years if the appropriate quotas were exhausted in the year of visa issuance. This is best illustrated by the fact that of 679,940 quota immigration visas issued by American consular officers abroad during this four-year period, 355,971 had to be charged against future quotas.

As a result of this requirement of the Displaced Persons Act and of other provisions of the immigration laws requiring that future quotas be charged, the future quotas of some twenty-five countries have been preempted up to 50 per cent of their annual volume. . . . Unless Congress should decide to wipe out these charges to future quotas it is safe to predict that quota immigration from these countries will remain at a low level.

The . . . principle which has significantly influenced the volume of immigration today is that of our good neighbor policy under which the law accords nonquota status to natives of independent countries of the Western Hemisphere, their husbands, wives and children. This provision which permits immigration from these countries without numerical limitation, has led in recent years to an increase in the immigration from the Western Hemisphere from some 22,000 in 1945 to close to 79,000 in 1954. This trend has been most marked during the last three years with an increase from 48,000 in 1952 to 59,000 in 1953 and to almost 79,000 in 1954. This recent increase is believed at least in part due to the fact that the Immigration and Nationality Act of 1952 does not carry over the contract labor law provisions of the Immigration Act of 1917. That Act prohibited the immigration of an alien who had contracted for or had manual employment promised to him. Consequently, during the last two years many immigrants, particularly from Mexico, could enter the United States on the basis of contracts of employment. Without affidavits of support from relatives these would have been barred from admission under the old law. . . .

The Immigration and Nationality Act provides that 50 per cent of each quota is made available first to skilled aliens whose services are urgently needed in the United States. During the fiscal year 1954, 2,456 skilled immigrants were admitted to the United States.

If a skilled alien is chargeable to an open quota his prospective employer will most likely suggest that he apply for a readily available nonpreference quota visa rather than apply for a first preference quota visa. In the case of an open quota a first preference quota visa would be of no benefit to the visa applicant but would entail additional procedures and expenses for his sponsor. The first preference quota provision is of considerable importance, in the case of small and over-subscribed quotas, since it enables an American employer to expedite the admission of a skilled alien whose services are needed in the United States.

If we examine the movement of visitors and other nonimmigrants coming each year to the United States, we can either count the number of visas issued to them by American consular officers abroad or the number of entries made by nonimmigrants at ports of entry as reported by the Immigration and Naturalization Service. We gain a full picture of the volume of the nonimmigrant movement only if we look at both figures. In so doing we must remember that a nonimmigrant visa frequently is valid for two years and for an unlimited number of entries into the United States. A visa issued in one year may be the basis for several admissions within a twenty-four month period. On the other hand, in evaluating the data on entries by nonimmigrants we must remember that they constitute a count of each entry even if made by the same person. In evaluating the figures on visas issued we must also remember that a large segment of nonimmigrants are exempted from the visa requirements.

With this in mind let us examine the available statistical data. The number of nonimmigrant visas issued abroad by consular officers during the last decade increased from 205,901 in the fiscal year 1945 to an all-time high of 400,001 in 1954. The 400,000 visas issued during the fiscal year 1954 constitute an increase of more than fifty thousand over the year 1953 and of more than eighty thousand compared with 1952, the fiscal year before the Immigration and Nationality Act became effective.

Thus it appears that the Immigration and Nationality Act stimulated rather than restricted the flow of nonimmigrants to the United States. If we examine the number of entries made by all classes of nonimmigrants we find that it has also continuously increased during the last ten years, and during the fiscal year 1954 reached 59,714,754, the high point for this period. This number includes some 24 million entries made by Canadian citizens and some 34 million entries by Mexicans.

The Immigration and Nationality Act emphasizes the doctrine of reciprocity as an important factor in the formulation of our policy regarding nonimmigrants. This means that certain controls on the movement of nonimmigrants are governed by the way in which foreign countries treat American citizens visiting them. For example the law requires that the fee charged an alien for a nonimmigrant visa should correspond to the fee charged an American citizen for a comparable visa by the country of the alien's nationality. If a given country charges an American citizen $75 for a visa as a temporary worker, the law requires that we also charge $75 to a national of that country coming to us as a temporary worker. If that country decides to lower or eliminate the visa fee for American citizens, we will automatically by administrative action lower or eliminate the fee charged to its nationals.

The principle of reciprocity also applies to the period of validity of a nonimmigrant visa and to the number of entries to which its bearer is entitled. If a foreign country issues to American citizens visas valid for twenty-four months and an unlimited number of entries, we will do likewise for nationals of that country who wish to visit our shores. If the foreign country, however, limits the validity of a visa issued to an American citizen to one month and to a single entry so will we do to that country's citizens. Under existing regulations, the maximum period for which a nonimmigrant visa may be issued is twenty-four months. . . .

If reciprocity exists the Secretary of State and the Attorney General are authorized by law to waive the nonimmigrant visa and passport requirements in the case of nationals of foreign contiguous territory and of adjacent islands. Under this authority the visa and passport requirements have been waived for the benefit of citizens of Canada. The visa requirement has been waived in the case of certain British subjects residing in Bermuda. The Department is presently exploring whether, under existing statutory authority and on the basis of reciprocity, it would be in best interests of the United States to waive nonimmigrant visas for nationals of other countries.

IMMIGRATION POLICY VERSUS FOREIGN POLICY [6]

American foreign policy is compounded of many ingredients. One of these ingredients is the voice of the President. To the President, under our Constitution, there is delegated the responsibility of giving executive direction to our foreign affairs. What he says, therefore, determines, in large part, the pattern of our relations with other nations. Then there is the voice of the Secretary of State, and the policies initiated by him, in collaboration with the President. Then there is the Congress of the United States. The Senate can give or withhold its ratification of treaties. But both Houses of Congress, in the enactment of legislation, can be and often are powerful factors in the determination of foreign policy. Any Act of Congress that shapes, in part, our relations with other peoples is of enormous consequence to the peace and security of the United

[6] From "The Immigration and Nationality Act of 1952—What It Means in Terms of Our Foreign Policy and What It Means to Social Work," an address by Dr. Walter W. Van Kirk, director of the Department of International Affairs, National Council of the Churches of Christ in the U.S.A., delivered before the National Council of Social Work, Atlantic City, New Jersey, May 11, 1954. Reprinted from the text published by the Community Relations Service. 386 Fourth Avenue. New York 16. 1954. p 1-8. Permission to reprint has been granted by Dr. Van Kirk, and by the Community Relations Service. Responsibility for the material is solely that of the author.

States. Such a piece of legislation is the McCarran-Walter Immigration and Nationality Act. The consequences of this Act, in respect to American foreign policy, must be taken into account in evaluating the role and assessing the influence of the United States in the search for a just and durable peace.

Any act of Congress that gives offense to large segments of the free peoples of the world adversely affects American foreign policy. This is what the McCarran-Walter Act does. The disparity between American foreign policy, as defined by the White House and the State Department, and our immigration and nationality legislation is brought sharply into focus by Communist aggression in Asia and the efforts of the United States to resist and repel that aggression. It is one of the primary aims of our foreign policy to prevent the imposition on Asia of the political system of Communist Russia and its Chinese Communist ally. Failure to achieve this aim would be, in the words of Secretary of State Dulles "a grave threat to the whole free community." To meet the threat posed by communism in Asia, the United States has asserted itself with vigor and determination. It bore aloft the flag of freedom in Korea. In that wartorn land there sleep thousands of American soldier dead. Incident to the Korean War our nation launched a program of military preparedness that has cost the American people many billions of dollars. Additional appropriations have been forthcoming for military and economic assistance to certain Asian countries. All for the purpose of stopping the spread of communism in Asia and thereby giving effect to one of the declared aims of American foreign policy.

More recently, Secretary of State Dulles, in an effort to meet the threat posed by communism in Asia, made a fervent plea for "united action." It may be assumed that what is meant by "united action" is cooperation by the free peoples of Asia with the free peoples of the Western world. Whether or not such "united action" will be achieved cannot at this moment be foreseen. It is clear, however, that the peace and security of the United States will be influenced, for weal or for woe, by the extent to which there can be achieved an identity of policies and procedures as between the freedom loving peoples of Asia and the Western world.

It is precisely at this point where the McCarran-Walter Act runs afoul American foreign policy. The plain truth is that this Act discriminates against Asiatics. This is true despite the fact that under this legislation Asiatics, albeit in small numbers, have been made eligible for United States citizenship. This was indeed a step forward by Congress. In other respects, however, as far as Asia is concerned, the Congress took a backward step. This backward step was taken when the Congress set up a racially conceived "Iron Curtain" known as the "Asia-Pacific Triangle." This Triangle includes, among others, the people of Afghanistan, Burma, China, Indonesia, Japan, Korea, India, and the Pacific Islands. Let it not be forgotten that in this area there lives half the population of the world. These people are peculiarly sensitive to the encroachments of what they describe as "American imperialism." They are in revolt against the second class status imposed upon them by those who exult in the doctrine of white supremacy. . . .

What does all this add up to? It adds up to this: Whereas President Eisenhower and the State Department are doing everything within their power to enlist the friendship and good will of the free people of Asia, the Congress, in the enactment of the McCarran-Walter Act, has done and is doing precisely the opposite of this. The President and the State Department look upon Asiatics as our equals when these people are asked to stand by our side for the preservation of freedom. The Congress, on the contrary, looks upon Asiatics as inferior to ourselves. If this conflict of policy is not apparent to the American people you can be sure it is apparent to the people of Asia. And to the Communists whose propagandists, day in and day out, tell the people of Asia that they are being discriminated against and insulted by the people and the Congress of the United States.

I labor this point respecting Asiatics for the simple reason that the United States is desperately in need of their friendship and good will, to say nothing of their raw materials which are an important factor in our stockpile of strategic materials. We of the United States comprise only 6 per cent of the world's population. . . . The people in the Asia-Pacific Triangle total 50 per cent. . . . It is not good manners nor good diplomacy, nor wise statesmanship, for the 6 per cent to hold in contempt the 50 per cent. It is also important to recall . . . that a new day has dawned for the people of Asia. They are no longer expendable. They deem themselves to be deserving of the respect of the West. Many of these Asiatic people have achieved national independence. Others of their number are moving in that direction. Their friendship cannot be bought with American dollars, nor rendered certain by American oratory. It is time the Congress of the United States woke up to this fact. It is time our lawmakers on Capitol Hill brought our immigration legislation respecting Asiatics into harmony with a foreign policy which presupposes the dignity and worth of Asia's millions. . . .

There is another point at which American immigration policy is in conflict with American foreign policy. I refer here to the North Atlantic Treaty Organization, and to the efforts initiated by our Government under this treaty to further the cause of European unity which unity is deemed by us to be an indispensable factor in preserving not only the peace of Europe but our own peace as well. One would suppose that those Europeans who are regarded by us as comrades in the common endeavor to establish the conditions of peace in Europe, and to withstand the pressures of Communist infiltration and aggression, would be accorded by our Congress a status of equality in its immigration legislation. Unhappily, this is not the case.

Turkey and Greece, for example, have been brought within the framework of the North Atlantic Treaty Organization. Both of these nations are important factors in the security arrangements to which the United States is a party. Turkey is also a vital connecting link between the West and the Near East. To keep Turkey and Greece within the orbit of the free world is one of the cardinal aims of American foreign policy. Yet in our immigration laws we arbitrarily assign to each of these nations a quota so small [225 and 308 respectively] as to suggest that their people, by contrast with the people of those European countries to which much larger quotas are assigned, are of an inferior order of human beings. The voice of American foreign policy, as set forth by the Executive branch of the Government, says to the Greeks and the Turks, "You are good enough to fight with us for the preservation of freedom," whereas the voice of the American Congress, as set forth in the McCarran-Walter Act, says to these same people: "You are less deserving than other people to live with us in the enjoyment of freedom." . . .

At a time when the President and the Secretary of State are striving to create a mutual security system in Europe which will have the effect of bridging some of the chasms by which Europeans in times past have been divided, the Congress superimposes upon that Continent its own lines of division between those Europeans deemed by our lawmakers to possess cultural refinements denied other Europeans. At a time when the President and the Secretary of State are striving to build a bridge of understanding and good will with which to span the chasm between Asiatics and Americans, and thereby tear down the wall of partition between East and West, the McCarran-Walter Act causes to be drawn upon the Asian world a vast triangle of racial prejudice and discrimination.

It is devoutly to be hoped that the American people, before it is too late, will recognize that such leadership as is theirs among the nations derives not from guns and bayonets and bombs, but from their historic witness in support of the rights and freedoms of mortals. There was a time when our Declaration of Independence and our Bill of Rights were the inspiration of millions. The downtrodden and oppressed of every land had looked toward our Statue of Liberty as the symbol of their hopes and aspirations. Subject and dependent peoples had looked to the United States as the champion and defender of political self-determination and independence. Always and everywhere our country had been equated with human rights and fundamental freedoms. Pilgrims in flight from tyranny had seen in the United States a haven of emancipation. Today, our economic and military strength is acknowledged by nations large and small. But industrial assembly lines with their shining gadgets, and hydrogen bombs with their mushroom clouds of radioactive poison will not suffice to save us once we have forfeited the confidence of peoples near and far in our moral integrity. . . .

Senator McCarran was of the opinion that the Act that bears his name is "tough on Communists." The very reverse is true. The people of the United States do not practice "toughness" in relation to the Communists when the Congress enacts legislation that is discriminatory in character and that divides the peoples of the earth by iron curtains of race and nationality. The people of the United States can practice "toughness" toward the Communists by walking in the paths of justice, freedom, and fair play, and by preserving for future generations the ideals of human worth and dignity that have enriched our American tradition.

It may be possible to contain communism by guns and bombs and threats of massive retaliation. But communism can be conquered only by ideas that transcend in spiritual import the ideas of the Kremlin. Such ideas are not the racist views reflected in certain provisions of the McCarran-Walter Act, but the ideas that exalt the worth of the individual and the oneness of humanity. So it was that President Eisenhower in his State of the Union Message, in 1953, requested the Congress to review the McCarran-Walter Act and "to enact a statute that will at one and the same time guard our national interest and be faithful to our basic ideas of freedom and fairness to all."

Finally, any act of Congress that is conceived in fear, compromises American foreign policy. Such a piece of legislation is the McCarran-Walter Act. It was conceived in fear. Insofar as is humanly possible subversives—and by subversives is meant not only Communists, but Nazi and Fascist subversives—must be prevented from coming to our shores. We love our land and the American way of life is treasured by us and for its preservation we are prepared both to live and to die. But when fear, unreasoned fear of communism dictates a law that is so obviously unfair to our many friends and allies, who, no less than we ourselves, are determined to resist communism to the death, the impact of American leadership is gravely weakened. The provisions of the McCarran-Walter Act respecting the granting of entry visas, and the procedures respecting deportation were written by a Congress with the jitters. . . . We who encourage others to be brave as they face the peril of communism act as though we were scared to death. We who call upon others to close their ranks in defense of freedom run hither and yon like frightened children utterly bereft that unity of purpose and endeavor by which national greatness is achieved.

There is found here the explanation of why it is that the United States is coming to be regarded as a nation of psychopaths. There can be no authoritative definition of American foreign policy until our Government is purged of the political upstarts who go about our land shouting their alarms, setting neighbor against neighbor, and paralyzing that moral initiative and creative endeavor by which, in times past, America achieved for itself a place of honor among the nations.

THE NEW LOOK IN AMERICAN IMMIGRATION [7]

Almost unnoticed by the general public . . . [the Immigration and Nationality Act of 1952] has brought about a number of changes which have proven beneficial to those who wish to come to the United States and have in many ways facilitated the administration of the law. . . . The new law tends to keep families united in migration, makes the use of quotas more flexible, and facilitates the admission of "new-seed immigrants." It gives due recognition to the need in the United States for certain skills, professional knowledge, and ability. It also opens the door to those who in the past were permanently barred for reasons of race or as a result of former and long past political affiliations. . . .

One of the most troublesome problems consular officers in the field and we in the Department of State had to deal with before the new law became effective was that of an American

[7] From "New Trends in American Immigration," an address by Edward S. Maney, director of the State Department's Visa Office, before the National Council on Naturalization and Citizenship, New York City, April 2, 1954. *United States Department of State Bulletin.* 30:599-602. April 19, 1954.

citizen who had married a woman of Asian ancestry and discovered only too late that under our laws then in existence he had only the choice between his country and his wife since our laws, with few exceptions, then did not permit the immigration of persons of Asian stock.

One of the most important changes the new law has brought about is the elimination of race as a bar to immigration. Alien wives and husbands of American citizens and alien children of American citizens are now eligible for immigration and entitled to nonquota status irrespective of their race. While it is true that the quotas accorded to Asian peoples are minimum quotas, it must be borne in mind that the volume of immigration from a given area is composed of both quota and nonquota immigrants and the latter group of course may exceed without limit the numerical limitations placed on quota immigrants. This is best illustrated by the fact that during the last fiscal year 1,043 Chinese and 2,489 Japanese came to the United States as immigrants, although Japan has a quota of only 185 and only 105 quota numbers are available to Chinese persons. . . .

Another important change which the new law has brought about is a general relaxation of the method by which the quota chargeability of an alien is determined. The basic rule remains unchanged that the quota of an alien is determined by his place of birth. While formerly only an alien wife chargeable to an oversubscribed quota could be charged to the more favorable quota of her accompanying husband, under the new law a husband as well as a wife may be charged to the more favorable quota of the accompanying spouse. For example, the Greek husband of an English woman may be charged to the quota of Great Britain. . . .

Another change relating to the quota chargeability has brought relief for many hardship cases for which there was no satisfactory solution under the old law. In a considerable number of cases prospective immigrants born in countries with small and oversubscribed quotas had to be given the discouraging information that they had to anticipate an indefinite waiting period under the quota of their country of birth although they had no tie to the country of their birth. . . . The law now permits that an alien who was born in a country in which neither of his parents was born and in which neither of his parents had a residence at the time of such alien's birth may be charged to the quota of either parent. . . . The alien born in India [of English missionary parents] may be charged to the British quota to which his parents would have been chargeable, and the alien who was born as son of the Swiss consul in Egypt may be charged to the quota of Switzerland.

Fuller use of existing quotas is made possible under the new law by permitting that any portion of a given quota not used during the first ten months of a quota year may be used without numerical limitation during May and June, that is, the last two months of the quota year. The restriction on the use of quotas to 10 per cent of each quota per month which now is applicable only during the first ten months applied to every month of the quota year under the old law. Thus, quota numbers were lost if a demand for immigration visas in excess of 20 per cent developed in May and June of a year under a quota which had not been utilized up to 80 per cent during the first ten months of the same quota year.

The prohibition against the immigration of manual labor, the so-called "contract labor provision" of the old law, by and large restricted immigration to the United States to relatives and close friends of American citizens and of permanent resident aliens. Aliens with good skills and many of them needed in this country but lacking family or friendship ties as a rule could not come to this country as they were unable to secure an acceptable affidavit of support as evidence that they were not likely to become public charges. Thus real "new-seed immigration" had become unknown in this country except for those immigrants who benefited under the Displaced Persons Act of 1948.

This situation has been drastically changed by two provisions of the new law. On one hand the outdated and inflexible contract labor law was eliminated. Now an alien is permitted to make arrangements for his employment before he comes to the United States and may submit evidence about his employment to show that he is not likely to become a public charge. Only if the Secretary of Labor certifies that there exists an oversupply of a given skill in a given locality of the United States will the immigration of aliens be barred who possess such skill and who are coming to this locality. . . .

The other provision of the new law which is helping the "new-seed immigrant" as well as American industry, business and cultural interests is the one giving a first claim to one half of the quota of each country to aliens whose services are needed urgently in the United States because of their high education, technical training, specialized experience, or exceptional ability and to their spouses and children.

The provision permitting immigrants to have employment before coming to the United States eventually will make itself felt also in the distribution of immigrants throughout the United States. As long as immigrants had to rely for their immigration on affidavits of support from relatives and friends in this country, the traditional trend of the immigrant movement continued to be to urban areas where there was already considerable immigrant settlement. Now it is to be expected that the settlement of new immigrants in the United States will not only be influenced by their tendency to go where they have friends or relatives but that it will be guided by job opportunities throughout the country.

Some misunderstanding seems to exist in the mind of the general public as to the effect the new law has had on the security provisions applicable to immigrants. The opinion seems to be widespread that the new law is more exacting in that respect. Actually the reverse is true.

For all practicable purposes the new law has reenacted the security provisions which had been part of the immigration laws since the passage in 1950 of the [McCarran] Internal Security Act. One significant change, however, has taken place. In the past, and ever since 1940, not only present but also former members of proscribed organizations were excluded from admission into the United States as immigrants. For example, an alien who in his youth some twenty or thirty years ago was a member of the Communist party was still ineligible to receive a visa regardless of the fact that long since he had given up his early political associations and had since become an outspoken fighter against communism.

The new law contains an escape clause for former voluntary members of proscribed organizations, a fact which has been given little if any publicity. The defector clause contained in the new law permits the issuance of a visa to a former voluntary member of a proscribed organization if the alien since the termination of his membership and for at least five years before the date of his visa application has been actively opposed to the principles and ideology of the proscribed organization of which he was a member.

This provision of law has made it possible to admit to the United States as immigrants a number of aliens whose record of the past years has justified that the United States show forgiveness for past political association and has thus enabled us at least indirectly to encourage future defections.

I know that some . . . are critical of the basic philosophy of our immigration laws, particularly its national-origins quota system, which actually goes back to the Immigration Act of 1924. In all fairness to the new law, this criticism I think should be divorced from a recognition of the fact that the new law has brought many important improvements over the old law, particularly in relation to its treatment of immigrants.

In their administration, laws can be interpreted literally and restrictively. On the other hand, they can be given a reasonable and humane interpretation. I want you to know that ever since the Immigration and Nationality Act has become effective we in the Visa Office have made every effort, without doing violence to the plain intent of the law, to interpret it reasonably and humanely. . . .

Although I am not speaking here for the Immigration and Naturalization Service, I am certain I can say both for that service and for the Department of State that we have done everything and will continue to do everything possible to interpret and administer the immigration laws consistent with the intent of Congress and in the best interest of the United States.

INJUSTICES OF THE McCARRAN-WALTER LAW [8]

Our present immigration law contains many provisions that deprive citizens and aliens alike of their just rights. These provisions are, it is believed, arbitrary, unnecessary to our security and well-being, and unfair. . . .

Exclusion

The applicant for an immigration visa has no legal rights, and it is certainly within our province to select only those whom we feel to be desirable. But such a statement, while in accord with the legalities of the situation, does not justify the use of arbitrary and despotic methods in selecting those to be admitted.

Since 1941 we have had the undemocratic procedure of excluding people without a hearing. This practice, it is true, was instituted to keep out spies and saboteurs. However, it has been more generally used to keep out people against whom there is some doubt, without giving them any opportunity to clarify their position. It has been used to keep out bona fide refugees, to separate families, and to exclude GI brides. Continuance of such a procedure can only encourage the opinion abroad that our consular officials are arbitrary and dictatorial.

Another provision of the immigration law denies visas to those convicted of two or more nonpolitical crimes with jail terms adding up to five years. Such persons are barred whether or not the offenses involved "moral turpitude." This provision differs markedly from former requirements that debarred aliens for actions involving moral turpitude. Previously, determination of what constituted moral turpitude was left to the American officials and American courts. This new provision implies acceptance of the verdict of foreign courts and does not take cognizance of the fact that under totalitarian regimes political opponents are often framed on nonpolitical charges.

[8] From *Paths To The New World: American Immigration—Yesterday, Today and Tomorrow,* pamphlet by Edward Corsi, state government official and former United States Immigration commissioner. (Freedom Pamphlet Series) Anti-Defamation League of B'nai B'rith. 212 Fifth Avenue. New York 10. 1953. p27-36. Reprinted by permission.

Conviction for any violation of law is sufficient—listening to the Voice of America, providing religious instruction to children in an Iron Curtain country, obtaining food without a ration card. Indeed, it has been pointed out that, if strictly construed, this provision would bar the admission of Cardinal Mindszenty on the ground that Communist Hungary had convicted him of two nonpolitical charges: neglecting to report foreign exchange transactions and speculating in currency. . . .

Also, to be excluded are those who misrepresent facts on travel or other documents. By this means, persons may be barred who, as the only means of saving their lives, were forced to conceal the truth as to their place of origin or former residence. This they may have done so as not to be forced back behind the Iron Curtain—or they may have wished to avoid reprisals against relatives. No desire to evade the quota or other provisions of the immigration law need be involved. . . .

Deportation

It is a fundamental maxim of American law that the same individual shall not be both prosecutor and judge. Under the 1952 law, the normal practice in deportation cases is to have the entire proceeding conducted by representatives of the Attorney General. Agents of the Attorney General make the investigation. Other members of the same agency present the case, and others still, hear it and make a decision. This combination of enforcement and judicial functions within one agency violates the principle of a fair hearing.

It should also be pointed out that the decision of the Attorney General is final in determining whether an alien should be deported or not. No court review is possible with respect to his decision. The only review permitted is under a habeas corpus proceeding after the alien has been taken into custody. However, this is possible only to determine the legality of the proceedings leading to his detention, but it cannot affect the administrative findings one way or the other.

Other provisions of the current law relating to deportation are unnecessarily severe. Prior to 1952, immigrants were protected against deportation for past acts on the basis of the statute of limitations. This required the action to be brought within five years. Aliens may now be deported for acts committed by them twenty to thirty years ago—acts which may not even have been deportable offenses when they were committed. . . .

Technical violation of any provisions regarding entry, even though the alien is blameless, is sufficient to require the Attorney General to deport the alien. An alien's failure to notify the Attorney General of his change of address may result in arrest and deportation proceedings. Past membership or affiliation in organizations now deemed subversive, no matter how innocent such membership was at the time, also subjects him to deportation. This penalty may be applied no matter how far removed in the past his membership may have been, no matter what his moral worth may be today.

Provision is made for the deportation of certain types of aliens without a hearing, and for the first time in our history, authority is granted to enter a deportation order in absentia.

Many of these provisions are excessively severe and have little to do with protecting our security. An alien who has legally entered the United States should thereafter be subjected to deportation only if his original entry was based upon fraud. If he misconducts himself, he should be tried and punished in the same manner as any other citizen. Certainly the misconduct of a youth or adult who was admitted at age five cannot be attributed to his country of origin but rather to conditions which exist in our own society. Deportation procedures in all cases should be just and fair. There should be a complete separation of those who investigate and prosecute and those who sit in judgment; and there should be adequate right of appeal. These requirements are closer to the American way of doing things.

Escapees

The new law rightfully bars the admission of spies and saboteurs. It also shuts the door on members of subversive organizations (or affiliates thereof), in order to assure the security of the United States. These sections of the law have at least two important defects. Honestly reformed ex-Communists, who have seen the folly of Communist ways, are excluded unless they are able to show a record of five years of active opposition to communism or fascism before becoming eligible for admission. This requirement makes it impossible to provide refuge for many honest opponents of Communist tyranny. It is inconsistent with the need to provide for such persons in our national interest.

Equally important is the unwarranted distinction made between Communist and Fascist totalitarianism. Communists, as part of a world movement to overthrow governments, are excluded. Nazis and Fascists, despite the lessons of current history, are assumed, under the act, to leave their totalitarian ideas behind them, on emigrating. They are permitted to enter this country. Dictatorships of any variety are a menace to freedom and democracy. It is doubtful that a person with the mentality that produced a Hitler or a Stalin will make a good American citizen. A law which protects America from one such enemy, without protecting against the other, makes little sense.

Second-class Citizens

. . . Naturalized citizens are subject to many penalties from which native-born Americans remain free. The McCarran-Walter Act contains provisions which bluntly impress on the naturalized American a brand of second-class citizenship. Thus, the accident of birth takes precedence over the individual rights of man.

A native-born citizen, for instance, is free to join any legitimate organization, without having to worry too much about possible results. A naturalized citizen, however, joins an organization at the risk of possible disaster. An example: A naturalized citizen may join a garden club in his area. Unknown to him, this club has been infiltrated by Communists, who have been using it as a "front" organization. The naturalized citizen faces the danger of denaturalization and deportation.

Another example: There are persons born in the United States whose parents come from countries in which the law vests the parents' nationality in the children, no matter where they are born. If such a person, after his twenty-second birthday, were to spend three years in the country of his parents' origin, he may, with certain exceptions, lose his United States citizenship. Thus, someone born here, who may have lived here most of his life, is treated differently from other citizens. No person can serve two masters at the same time, and it is not in our national interest to permit retention of dual nationality. But Americans who have been born here, and resided in this country till maturity, may be assumed to have elected American citizenship. They should be entitled to the same treatment as any other citizens. . . .

The Rights of Citizens

Our present immigration law legalizes procedures which, although aimed at the apprehension and deportation of aliens illegally in the United States are couched in such broad terms that they endanger the civil rights even of native-born citizens. For example: an immigration officer may, under the law, interrogate any person whom he believes to be an alien, as to his right to remain in the United States. Such a person may be visited at any hour of the day or night for questioning, without a warrant. Another provision of the present law along the same lines permits any immigration officer to search any car or other conveyance within twenty-five miles of any external boundary of the country. There is no requirement that probable cause be shown for such search, nor is a warrant necessary.

The possibilities of abuse in such provisions are great. During the Palmer raids of 1920, thousands of people, citizens and non-citizens, were arrested without a warrant in illegal raids. Those who remember that period cannot view with equanimity the legalization of such procedures. [Alexander Mitchell Palmer was Attorney General 1919-1921. His raids on offices and members of the Workers' party (later the Communist party) and other suspected subversives were of doubtful legality and were marked by mass arrests and mass deportations. They lasted for six months in 1919-1920.—Ed.]

Loss of Citizenship

One of the peculiar characteristics of our immigration laws is the numerous grounds provided for loss of citizenship through expatriation. We now have more such grounds for revoking citizenship than has any other country in the world. Ten different grounds are provided, such as treason, desertion in time of war, obtaining naturalization in a foreign state upon application, renunciation of American citizenship. These, and similar grounds based on unwillingness to accept the responsibilities of citizenship, are traditional causes for expatriation.

Among the remaining reasons are several which have deprived Americans of citizenship as a result of acts which hardly warrant such a penalty.

For example, service in the armed forces of a foreign state: this may now cause loss of citizenship even though the nationality of the foreign state is not acquired and no oath of allegiance is taken. This may result even if there has been no act inconsistent with the duties and obligations of an American citizen. Thus, Americans who volunteered for service in the armies of Canada and Great Britain during the late war, in a cause entirely consistent with allegiance to the United States, would under our present law be subjected to loss of citizenship.

Another illustration is the loss of citizenship for voting in a foreign political election. Some years ago, for example, thousands of letters were written to Italian citizens by their American relatives urging them to vote on the side of democracy and against the Communist candidates. All qualified persons were urged to vote, including American citizens of dual nationality living in Italy at the time. The Communists were defeated. Only a special law passed by Congress preserved the citizenship of these Americans. Without that law, they now would be faced with loss of their most precious possession for their service in the cause of freedom. . . .

Professors and Scientists

The 1952 immigration law throws up complex "paper roadblocks" to hinder the admission both of scientists who wish to come here as temporary visitors and those who seek permanent admission.

In the case of temporary visitors, this is done by carrying over the provisions of the Internal Security Act of 1950. This Act set up a cumbersome, tedious, and uncertain process of screening visitors. Under this procedure, even if they are to be in the United States for only a single day, professors and scientists must satisfy substantially all the health, financial, security and other requirements that apply to permanent immigrants. The National Science Foundation has estimated that at least 50 per cent of all foreign scientists who apply for entry into the United States experience difficulties or delays.

This red tape has had a threefold effect. It has hampered the free exchange of information on which much of our scientific progress is based. In this connection, it must be remembered that it is only because we were able to draw on the scientific knowledge of all the world that we were able to develop such wonders as atomic energy, jet aircraft, and penicillin. Secondly, it has alienated distinguished citizens of friendly foreign countries who have been embarrassed by the long drawn out investigations. These persons have almost invariably been given visas. But it is of little value to be permitted to enter the country in December to present a paper that was to have been delivered in July. Thirdly, it has caused international scientific societies to transfer to other countries, such as Canada, meetings that were originally scheduled for the United States.

Professors and scientists who wish to come to this country to live here permanently are also faced with new barriers. Formerly, they were entitled to nonquota status if they had been teaching for at least two years preceding their visa application. Under the 1952 law they no longer have nonquota status, but may qualify only for first preference quota status as "skilled aliens."

For example, if Enrico Fermi, the refugee Italian scientist who played a crucial role in the development of atomic energy during the war wanted to come to this country for permanent residence today [1953], he would have to . . . obtain a clearance from the United States Employment Service; get written statements from labor organizations; submit affidavits of persons having special knowledge of him; assemble clippings of advertisements for persons, in the United States, to perform the services which he claims to be able to render; produce copies of his diplomas, school certificates, and other similar documents. Then he would be placed on a waiting list. . . .

Racial Discrimination

The new immigration law of 1952 eliminates race, as such, as a reason for exclusion. It then proceeds to single out Orientals for special prejudicial treatment on the basis of racial ancestry. This it does by providing that any person, no matter where born, "attributable by as much as one-half of his ancestry" to peoples native to the Asia-Pacific zones, is chargeable to the extremely limited quotas of these Oriental lands. Thus, a person born in England of an English father and a Chinese mother would be charged to the negligible China quota. No other group is similarly treated.

Racial bias is also indicated in the establishment of subquotas of 100 for immigrants born in the colonies or dependent areas of the Western Hemisphere. While it has been said that this provision applies to whites and Negroes alike, the principal effect is to exclude from this country Negroes from the Caribbean Islands. It makes a particularly drastic cut in the immigration of Negroes from the British West Indies, notably Jamaica. Heretofore these persons were assigned to the large quotas of their mother countries. . . .

One of the more pointed commentaries on the racial features of the Act is contained in a letter addressed to Senator Humphrey of Minnesota, during the debates which preceded passage of the Act. It was signed by five representatives of American Indian tribes. It read, in part:

Dear Senator Humphrey:

As America's only nonimmigrants, we would like to go on record as being opposed to the major aspects of the McCarran immigration bill. . . . We are against this bill because of its basic philosophy . . . which accepts and provides for the continuance of racial discrimination. To this we are unalterably opposed. . . .

As American Indians we are not immediately threatened by laws to stop immigration and to deport men and women born abroad. Sometimes we wish we had established such a law in 1492. . . .

IV. THE OUTLOOK

EDITOR'S INTRODUCTION

Since its passage, as before, the McCarran-Walter Act has been subjected to a great deal of criticism, a great deal of praise, and a great many efforts to change or supplement its provisions. These efforts have been made within Congress, as described below in "Time For A Change?", and without, and one of them culminated in the successful passage of the Refugee Relief Act of 1953.

The Refugee Relief Act, with its statutory termination at the end of 1956, was admittedly a stopgap measure and was accepted as a compromise by opponents of the immigration act it was designed to ameliorate. The nature of this compromise is discussed by Cabell Phillips in "Compassion by Slide Rule," below, and the mixed reaction to both its provision and its administration is evident in the four concluding articles of this section. Efforts to liberalize and extend it—failing revision of the McCarran-Walter Act itself—will undoubtedly be made, for the economic and emotional questions raised by refugees will doubtless go unresolved for years.

Meanwhile, study of the basic problem of immigration continues, both here and abroad, for it is not ours alone, and a solution in keeping with our governmental processes and national character will eventually emerge. Canada's solution, described by Carleton Ketchum in "Canada's Welcome Mat," is obviously not for us, nor is that of other countries where the need for manpower is of pressing concern. We can study their solutions, but neither our political nor our economic condition permits us to use them as blueprints. All we can do is examine our own peculiar problems with clear and open minds as we join what Senator Lehman refers to below as the "struggle to provide the United States with a permanent, reasonable, and humanitarian immigration program."

TIME FOR A CHANGE? [1]

Numerous proposals have been made, in Congress and out-side, for removing rigidities of the national-origins system and what are regarded as unnecessary, unwise, and unjust discriminations. Some of these proposals may be cited.

The President's Commission

A President's Commission on Immigration and Naturalization was appointed [by President Truman] shortly after passage of the McCarran-Walter Act "to study and evaluate the immigration and naturalization policies of the United States" and to make recommendations "for such legislative, administrative, or other action, as in its opinion may be desirable in the interest of the economy, security, and responsibilities of this country." . . .

The seven persons appointed were a former Solicitor General of the United States (as chairman), a former United States Commissioner of Immigration and Dean of the University of Pennsylvania Law School, a former General Counsel of the Atomic Energy Commission, the Chairman of the Board of Immigration Appeals in the Department of Justice, and three members eminent in the Lutheran, Roman Catholic, and Friends groups.

This Commission, of course, had the benefit of the extensive testimony given at the joint hearings of the congressional subcommittees, the competing measures offered by other members of Congress, and the extensive discussion in the press and in forums that had preceded and followed the enactment of the McCarran-Walter Act. They also held hearings in eleven cities across the country. The record of oral testimony given in these hearings by some four hundred persons and the written statements submitted by 234 persons make up a volume of about 2,100 pages, published by the Judiciary Committee of the House

[1] From *As We Do Unto Others*, booklet by Charles H. Seaver, writer and editorial consultant for the Department of International Justice and Goodwill, National Council of the Churches of Christ in the U.S.A. The Department. 120 East 23d Street. New York 10. 1952. p 11-26. Permission to reprint is granted by Mr. Seaver, who originally wrote this material for the Department of International Justice and Goodwill of the National Council of the Churches of Christ in the U.S.A. Responsibility for the material in the booklet is solely that of the author.

of Representatives. The views of private individuals, of agents of Federal, state, and municipal governments, and of representatives of many religious, political, and social organizations were obtained and included. The report of the Commission was made January 1, 1953, and was published as a book of about 340 pages under the title *Whom We Shall Welcome.*

The recommendations of the Commission as to the national-origins quota system were that it should be abolished and that a "unified quota" system be substituted. This "contemplates a maximum annual number of quota immigrants, to be determined by the Congress, and a flexible method of allocating visas within the annual maximum. Visas should be allocated on the basis of statutory categories best serving the interests of the United States, and without regard to national origin, race, color, or creed. This allocation of percentages to these categories should be made periodically by an administrative agency, established for that and other purposes, and would be subject to review by the President and the Congress."

The "categories" substituted for national-origin quotas would be (1) refugees (such as have been included in special legislation); (2) "immigrants whose admission would result in uniting families"; (3) "persons of skills and occupations to fill needs certified by the . . . appropriate officials to be necessary in or desirable for the national welfare"; (4) "persons from countries of the free world where immigration to the United States can meet special needs and can provide substantial alleviation of hardships which threaten economic, political, and social stability in those countries"; (5) "general immigration of all other qualified persons, without regard to national origin, race, color, or creed." No priorities among these categories are suggested; but the total number admissible annually would be a maximum fixed by Congress—just as a maximum of 155,000 (theoretically) was set for the national-origins quotas. The Commission favored a maximum of about 250,000 annually, which would be one sixth of 1 per cent of the whole population of the United States according to the most recent census (rather than of the white population in 1920). There has been fairly general agreement among experts in government agencies, other students of population trends, leaders of labor, and the major religious bodies that the annual admission of at least this number of immigrants is desirable and will add to the resources of the nation.

New Omnibus Bill

A new omnibus immigration and naturalization bill, introduced in . . . [August 1953] by a group of eight senators and twenty-four representatives, would repeal the present Act. [Commonly called the Lehman Bill, after Senator Herbert H. Lehman, Democrat, New York, one of its sponsors, it is officially S. 2585. Because House procedure requires that each sponsor introduce his own bill, the corresponding bill numbers in the House are H.R. 6820 to H.R. 6843 inclusive.—Ed.] It incorporates, however, the substance or the letter of . . . [the McCarran-Walter Act's] less controversial provisions, with clarification and simplification of many of the "legal jungles." It offers a substitute for the national-origins quota system, not unlike the recommendation of the President's Commission, but with detailed specifications. The substitute is called a "unified quota system."

This bill sets the total annual quota immigration at one sixth of 1 per cent of the population of the United States at the last census: 251,000 annually. But it includes the Western Hemisphere within the quota system; so the total is probably not much greater than the theoretical maximum set in the present quota system plus the present legal Western Hemisphere immigration.

The basis of selection, within this limit of numbers, has no reference to race, color, religion, or national origin. The following preferences are stated, with a range flexible according to administrative judgment each year: to unite families of citizens and resident aliens, 25-35 per cent; for special skills, technical knowledge, education, and potential contribution to national security, 5-10 per cent; for refugees from persecution or oppression, 15-25 per cent; to alleviate acute political and economical problems, including displacement, 20-25 per cent; for others, "first come, first served," but not more than 10 per cent; to any nationality, not more than 20 per cent. The "security" provisions of the Act of 1952 are retained, with no changes affecting their efficiency.

The authors of this bill say it is the product of eight months or more of drafting by experts in this field; with study of the arguments and proposals included in the hearings on the previous legislation and those held by the President's Commission, besides a vast amount of other discussion before and since the passage of the McCarran-Walter Act. Its substitute for the national-origins quota system deserves serious thought and full discussion by people representing various points of view. It provides one carefully considered answer to those who may have some misgivings about the national-origins quota system but ask, "What other system of selection is practicable?" And many of the changes suggested by critics of the present act appear here in legal form.

The President's Recommendations

President Eisenhower, in his State of the Union Message (February 2, 1953), stated that "existing legislation" regarding aliens and naturalized citizens "contains injustices," and requested that a statute be enacted "which will at one and the same time guard our legitimate national interest and be faithful to our basic ideas of freedom and fairness to all." Subsequently, in a letter to Senator Watkins (April 6) for transmission to the Senate Commission on the Judiciary, he suggested that a study of the operation of many of the administrative provisions of the Act of 1952 should be immediately undertaken, and cited these provisions for study:

"The provisions which make inadmissible any alien who, in the opinion of the consul, is likely to become a public charge at any time in the future. This places upon the consul the burden of forecasting events which cannot be predicted and, it is claimed, would permit abuse of discretionary judgment.

"The provisions which make ineligible for a visa any alien with respect to whom the consular officer knows or has reasonable ground to believe he probably would, after entry, engage in espionage, sabotage, or 'subversive' activities. It is asserted that this provision vests in the consul the authority, without restraint, to determine by his own mental processes the probability of future proscribed conduct, thus permitting a possible abuse of discretionary judgment.

"The provision which permits an immigration official to interrogate without warrant 'any alien or person believed to be an alien as to his right to be or to remain in the United States.' It is said that unless the word 'believed' is clarified so as specifically to require 'probable cause,' an abuse of this authority could possibly subject any citizen to improper interrogation.

"Provisions under which, it is asserted, naturalized citizens have only 'second class' citizenship because they, as distinguished from native-born citizens, can be expatriated because of residence abroad for certain periods of time, without reference to any other conduct on their part.

"New restrictions upon granting leave to seamen while ships are in United States ports.

"The provision which exempts from the criminal grounds of exclusion those aliens who have been convicted abroad of purely political offenses fails to define the term 'political.' It is asserted that it is therefore difficult for administrative officers to determine whether the 'criminal' offenses for which individuals have been convicted are indeed of a criminal, as distinguished from a political, nature.

"The provisions permitting aliens who were and are believers in nazism and fascism to enter the United States unless it can be affirmatively shown that they advocated the establishment of those ideologies in the United States.

"Deportation provisions that permit an alien to be deported at any time after entry, irrespective of how long ago he was involved, after entry, in an activity or affiliation designated as 'subversive.' Such alien is now subject to deportation even if his prior affiliation was terminated many years ago and he has since conducted himself as a model American.

"The provision which authorizes the Attorney General to suspend deportation of certain deportable aliens if 'exceptional and extremely unusual hardship' is demonstrated. It is asserted, however, that these restrictive terms are not explained in the law, thus leaving the interpretation of the phrase open to administrative determination, subject to Congressional approval or 'veto.' It is argued that the law should more clearly state the standards upon which this discretionary relief may be granted by the Attorney General.

"The provisions which permit the continuation of up to a 50 per cent mortgage extending far into the future on the quotas of many countries. . . ."

The Refugee Act of 1953

This Act . . . (Public Law 203), urged by the President as an emergency measure, authorized the admission of 209,000 refugees, expellees, and escapees from communism over a three-year period as nonquota immigrants. It specified a maximum of 55,000 of German ethnic origin and 35,000 of whatever ethnic origin formerly resident in Communist-dominated or Communist-occupied areas of Europe and now harbored in West Germany, West Berlin, or Austria; 45,000 of Italian ethnic origin (including refugees from former Italian colonies) now in Italy or Trieste; 15,000 of Greek ethnic origin now in Greece; 15,000 of Dutch ethnic origin now in the Netherlands. Another allotment of 15,000 was for persons of Italian origin in Italy or Trieste who have near relatives in the United States. Smaller allotments to various groups made up the remaining 29,000. (A provision was added for 5,000 in adjustments of status.)

Visas were to be granted only to those applicants who met the security requirements of the Immigration and Nationality Act of 1952 (after thorough investigation as to each applicant by American officials abroad), and also had individual sponsors in the United States of proven responsibility who would assure that the refugees would not become economic risks. Besides the information required from and about the refugee, the Administrators of the Act required each sponsor to fill out an elaborate form containing not only his assurances but also information as to his property, income, bank account, taxes paid, etc. . . .

Whatever may be the working of this emergency legislation, administered in the framework of the basic Act of 1952, the refugee problem will doubtless continue for some years. It requires international cooperation, whether through the United Nations or other international channels. Other nations have followed our lead in this regard when we have led—as when we were doing our part in 1950-52 under special legislation. It has become obvious, however, that only revision of our basic law, to make it flexible in accordance with changing conditions and needs, will permit effective exercise of our responsibility and bring about effective international cooperation.

If these suggestions for congressional study of the McCarran-Walter Act of 1952 have been seriously entertained, no amending legislation has emerged . . . perhaps because both congressional and public attention has been diverted to other issues. The Emergency Refugee Act of 1953 was only a temporary measure, involving no revision of the basic law.

The substitute bill introduced by a number of Democratic senators and representatives . . . has reposed on the shelves of the Judiciary committees of both Houses. However . . . a bill [S. 3292, H.R. 8802] containing many amendments to the McCarran-Walter Act has been introduced in both Houses under Republican sponsorship (April 19, 1954). It follows generally the lines of President Eisenhower's recommendations.

As to the national-origins quota system, it would use the 1950 census rather than the 1920 census as a basis for quotas, remove certain provisions discriminating against Asiatic and colonial peoples, bar Fascists as well as Communists, and distribute unused quotas among nationalities with quotas of less than 7,000. (In the fiscal year 1953, over 57,000 quotas were unused.) As to other parts of the McCarran-Walter Act, it would remove certain provisions which create a "second-class citizenship" for naturalized Americans; establish a statute of limitations for aliens threatened with deportation; and set up a board of visa appeals in the State Department.

Whether or not [we adopt] amendments to the McCarran-Walter Act along either of these lines or along lines where the Democratic and Republican bills serve a similar purpose, depends upon the expression of public opinion. Neither bill would command the united support of the party to which its sponsors belong; but some bipartisan compromise may eventually be worked out—if the people show sufficient concern.

CANADA'S WELCOME MAT [2]

Canada, whose territory of 3,845,774 square miles exceeds that of the continental United States by 823,387 square miles but whose population remains equal only to that of New York State [about 15 million], seeks to increase her population within the next twenty years to 30 million citizens.

The advent of an era of aeronautical and atomic warfare that renders the country vulnerable to attack from the air by enemies has caused her population from the point of view of defense alone to become a matter of the utmost importance.

Quite apart from the factor of defense, however, Canada today is urgently in need of a greatly increased population. She requires that population to cope with problems created by her unprecedented industrial developments resulting chiefly from her surprising discoveries of rich mineral, oil and other resources and also to provide men and women to serve on the nation's 70,000 or more farmlands in a period in which Canadian agriculture is confronted with the most serious situation in its experience in respect of farm labor. . . .

For the foregoing reasons the government's recently formed Department of Citizenship and Immigration through its considerable number of immigration and settlement officers stationed throughout Europe has sought by every legitimate means within its power to bring about a population increase by large scale immigration.

That effort has resulted in the admission to this country since the ending of World War II of a million immigrants the majority of whom within five years of their arrival will have

[2] From "30,000,000 People by 1975?" by Carleton Ketchum, member of the Canadian House of Commons. *Monetary Times* [Toronto]. 122:22-6+. September 1954. Reprinted by permission.

qualified for the status of full citizenship. On May 1 [1954] the date upon which that one million figure was supposed to have been reached, the total admitted to the country is believed to have exceeded that number by several thousands while each succeeding month was expected to bring thousands of additional arrivals from the United Kingdom and various countries of Europe.

No limitation is placed upon the number of British, French or United States citizens who wish to settle in Canada. With those exceptions, however, the selective principle invariably applies. Applicants for immigration visas are thoroughly examined by the on-the-spot Canadian immigration officials located in the countries wherein their application was made. So searching, indeed, is that examination that during the fiscal year ended March 31, 1952, 20,883 persons who made applications in countries of Continental Europe were refused such visas.

Such a careful screening process obviously ensures that only the most desirable types of citizens are selected as acceptable immigrants. Thus the standard of these people is uniformly high. The consequence is that while many, including those who contracted loan obligations in respect of monies advanced for their passage, spend their first year or so working in a variety of menial categories of employment the majority, after the expiration of that period, graduate into spheres of employment more to their liking and for which, by virtue of their special qualifications, educational and cultural backgrounds they are better equipped to develop successful careers for themselves as New Canadians.

The fact is worthy of note that while 165,000 of the million immigrants admitted to Canada within the nine-year period since the ending of the Second World War were "displaced persons" the majority of that number were persons who had chosen to migrate to Canada not because they were destitute or without prospect of employment when they first came in contact with Canada's immigration officialdom but because they felt that Canada was a land of hope that offered them the prospect of a future of prosperity and happiness. In most cases these people were in employment when they applied for their immigration visas and possessed the necessary funds to finance their migration.

Most of the so-called "displaced persons" accepted for settlement in Canada became displaced when their homelands were invaded by the Communists. Unwilling to reconcile themselves to life under Red rule they fled or, when made captives of the Communists, contrived to escape. Then at the earliest opportunity they sought immigration facilities which enabled them to become established in what many since have been pleased to describe or regard as this Land of the Future.

Professions and trades for which many of the new citizens were either wholly or partially trained before their arrival in Canada extend in variety from the practice of law, medicine, chemistry, dentistry, engineering, architecture to teaching, painting, sculpturing and others of the arts including ballet and all branches of music, to bricklaying, carpentering and doing the work of the master or apprentice electrician.

The extent to which the Canadian Government has sought to increase selective immigration in recent years may be gauged from the fact that the Immigration branch of the Department of Citizenship and Immigration now maintains [nineteen] fully staffed offices abroad. . . . Immigration or settlement officers attached to those offices take advantage of every available opportunity to give lectures and show films intended to provide a true and unbiased picture of the Canadian way of life.

Canada Offers You New Opportunities in a Growing and Prosperous Land, proclaims a large colored poster embracing the Canadian Coat of Arms displayed by these settlement officers wherever they are stationed.

A plan described as a major development in the government's immigration policy was devised in December 1950 to provide financial aid to prospective immigrants on a recoverable basis to help defray the cost of their transportation to Canada. The advances were to apply to transportation from port of embarkation to destination in Canada. Immigrants accepting such assistance were required to agree to work for a Canadian employer and remain in the same type of employment until such time as the amount advanced had been repaid. The immigrant was further required to authorize his employer to deduct amounts from his wages until the loan had been liquidated while stipulation was added that the period of repayment must not exceed twenty-four months.

Many Canadian firms similarly have advanced funds to secure the services of skilled workers from abroad for their factories and their workshops. Yet another plan is that which permits the immigrant to travel to Canada in a Trans-Canada Air Line plane at a cost which to him must not exceed $160.00; the equivalent of the cost of tourist class passage by sea. The government pays the balance of the regular air fare to the air line company. That plan was adopted in the first instance to meet the contingency of a lack of available shipping in the North Atlantic which for a time became a factor in preventing many prospective immigrants from venturing upon their desired pilgrimage to this "Land of Opportunity."

Among unofficial organizations which have assisted in the movement of these new settlers, chiefly those of the category classified as "displaced persons" is the Canadian Christian Council for Re-settlement of Refugees. The Council was formed in June 1947, to aid in locating and "processing" approved immigrants from overseas who had become "displaced persons" but who did not fall into the category of persons eligible for the assistance of the International Refugee Organization. It is entirely a voluntary organization composed of the Catholic Immigrant Aid Society, the Canadian Mennonite Board of Education, the German Baptist Colonization and Immigration Society, Canadian Lutheran World Relief, the Sudeten Committee and the Latvian Relief Fund of Canada.

About 11,000 Dutch agriculturalists emigrated to Canada under a special arrangement with the Government of the Netherlands. They were not farm laborers but farm settlers possessed of financial resources who lost the use of their lands in Holland when they were flooded as a result of military operations during World War II.

Other similar arrangements facilitated the entry of a group of 4,327 Polish ex-servicemen who contracted to work on farms at the outset of their careers in Canada, 500 Maltese with their dependents whose passage was paid by the Government of Malta, settlers from India who were admitted at a quota rate of 150 per year for an indefinite period, 1,000 Catholic and 1,000 Jewish war orphans admitted by the government at the request of the Catholic Immigrant Aid Society and the Canadian Jewish Congress. . . .

The Canadian Chamber of Commerce, Canadian Manufacturers' Association and the Canadian Construction Association are among many national groups which have briefed the government in support of its continuance of an aggressive immigration policy. The Chamber of Commerce in its most recent brief urged the government to remember its policy enunciated prior to the Korean war when it declared that "in a world of shrinking distances and international insecurity we cannot ignore the danger that lies in a small population attempting to hold so great a heritage as ours." The Canadian Manufacturers' Association urges the government to establish the figure of 150,000 immigrants per year as its minimum rather than its maximum target; the Canadian Construction a policy that will ensure a large and steady influx of workers skilled in the construction and allied trades.

The Citizenship Branch of the Department of Citizenship and Immigration has secured excellent results in its efforts through provincial governments and such voluntary organizations as the Canadian Citizenship Council, Canadian Educational Association, Canadian Association for Adult Education and similar groups, to educate the new citizens and inculcate in them a sense of appreciation of the so-called Canadian way of life.

That governmental agency has organized evening classes directed on a voluntary basis by public-spirited educationalists with such success that scores if not hundreds of these newcomers, owing to the instruction they received, have qualified for scholarships and university degrees.

Illuminating filmstrips depicting life in Canada and the Canadian economy in all of its multifarious phases were prepared for the exclusive use of those voluntary instructors at their night classes. Supplementing those courses of instruction has been a vast quantity of literature inclusive of copies of such now well known booklets as those included in the Citizenship Series bearing the title of *Our Land, Our History, Our Government,* and *Our Resources.* That literature made available to all of them has considerably aided many thousands of these people to qualify for their Citizenship Certificate. . . .

The procedure applied to an immigrant seeking Canadian citizenship status is similar to that prevailing in the United States. He must file with the Clerk of the Court in the judicial district in which he lives a Declaration of Intention indicating his intention to become a Canadian citizen and reside permanently in Canada.

Before he can receive from the Court his Certificate of Citizenship, however, he must have completed five years of residence in Canada. He must have proven to the Court that he was legally admitted to the country. He must be a person of good character and satisfy the Court that he has acquired a speaking knowledge of the English or French language, and that he understands the responsibilities and privileges of Canadian citizenship. He must also provide a written declaration renouncing his foreign nationality and take an Oath of Allegiance to the Sovereign of the British Commonwealth of Nations as the Queen of Canada. . . .

Canada's present efforts to increase her population by immigration should not be construed as meaning that her larger population of the future will be produced alone by immigration. That increase, indeed, will depend to a large extent upon a natural increase in the prevailing population. For if that increase continues, an increase that stands at 18 per thousand to constitute the largest rate of natural increase in the nation's history, Canada's present population of 15 million will have a basic natural increase of 270,000 each year. Assuming that, as expected, immigration will continue at an average of 160,000 per annum, the combined increase of 430,000 each year will, or should by 1975—twenty-one years from now—result in the larger population of between 25 million and 30 million for which the nation has begun to plan.

THE WORLD'S UPROOTED [3]

The drying up of pasture land, floods and earthquakes, war, revolutions and religious crusades have from time immemorial sent men forth in quest of new homes. In our own time millions of people were uprooted by World War II, some fleeing before the advancing Nazi armies, others being sent by the Germans to fill slave-labor and concentration camps. With the collapse of Hitler's power, the victorious Russians, advancing west of the Dnieper behind the retreating Nazis, marched on into the Galician marshes whence Poles were uprooted only to move on into their newly acquired territories as far west as the Oder and the Niesse. The Germans thus dispossessed in their turn fanned out over Western Germany from Schleswig to Bavaria, and a few have already begun to find their way across the ocean to the United States.

Millions of people have been uprooted by economic pressures or natural calamities, such as famines in China and India, earthquakes in Assam and Peru, and dust storms in Oklahoma.

Far more significant in international politics are the innumerable victims of totalitarian regimes, religious persecutions, slave-labor recruitment and pogroms, or shifting political boundaries. The fate of these political refugees has embroiled the major powers of the world in acrimonious debate.

The problem of displaced persons has become so prevalent in our day that an Austrian official recently remarked, "This was to be the age of the Common Man. I think it is more likely to be known as the Age of the Refugee." To the average American, even though his own ancestors may have been among the millions of Europeans who sought sanctuary here, this statement may appear extreme. We tend to think that the European refugee problem is due to Nazi aggression and the results of World War II, and that the reestablishment of persons displaced by these recent events might dispose of the refugee problem.

[3] From "The World's Refugee Problem," by Fred W. Riggs, *Foreign Policy Reports* research associate. *Foreign Policy Reports.* 26:190-9. January 15, 1951. Reprinted by permission.

This, however, is not the case. There are in the world today between 30 and 60 million refugees. Their displacement is due to causes deeply rooted in the structure of modern society— among them the concepts of nationalism, democracy and popular citizenship, and the expansion of an industrial, mass-production economy—as well as to the social disorders produced by war and totalitarianism.

A glance at some of the world's chief refugee situations will illustrate the way in which these factors have interacted to displace millions of persons. Perhaps the largest number of refugees in any country is found in China, where as many as 50 million have been made homeless by war and civil strife. Presumably many have now been resettled, but information concerning the situation under Chinese Communist rule cannot be obtained. A group of about 17,000 European refugees (largely Jewish) found asylum in Shanghai before World War II, but most of them have now been relocated. The substantial Russian emigré community in China has been largely repatriated.

More than 12 million Moslems and Hindus who became ethnic minorities following the partition of India in 1947 were involved in one of the world's greatest and most bloody population exchanges. More recently communal disturbances in Bengal have involved several million more persons entering and leaving East Pakistan. Other millions are reported to have fled Kashmir, going to West Pakistan.

At the present time millions of Koreans uprooted by the Communist armies have tremendously aggravated the refugee problem in that battered peninsula. Perhaps half a million people have been displaced in Burma's many-sided civil war.

In the Middle East the influx of Jewish refugees to Palestine —the product of one of the world's most tragic "minority" problems—and the creation of the state of Israel caused some 800,000 Arabs to flee their homes. In Western Europe less than 80,000 Jewish DPs remain, but 800,000 Jews in Moslem countries and another 600,000 in Eastern Europe are furnishing new refugees who seek asylum in Israel.

In Western Europe there mingle layer upon layer of displaced persons, remnants of old groups mixing with new arrivals.

The oldest among them are the interwar refugees—White Russians, Armenians, Spanish Republicans, anti-Nazis and anti-Fascists, the by-product of civil wars, revolutions and ethnic persecutions. Perhaps 550,000 of these remained in the summer of 1947 from an original total of about two million.

A second layer consists of people uprooted as a direct result of German expansion—the "Displaced Persons" in a technical sense. These include prisoners of war taken by the Germans, political and racial victims in the concentration camps, and slave laborers brought to Germany. At the end of the war almost eight million such people were identified, but by the end of 1945 most of them had been repatriated. In the summer of 1947 less than a million remained, consisting largely of Eastern Europeans who were unwilling to return to areas under the control of the USSR.

A third layer of refugees were uprooted by the Axis defeat, chiefly some 12.5 million Germans, but 100,000 Italians and almost 6 million repatriated Japanese could be included in this category. Among the Germans may be distinguished four categories—the expellees, "refugees," infiltrees and evacuees. The expellees consist of Germans forcibly deported—in accordance with an inter-Allied plan—from their original places of residence in Eastern Europe or the parts of Germany taken over by Poland. An approximately equal number left either voluntarily or because of local pressure—exceeding the numbers approved under the Potsdam agreement—and are referred to as "refugees."

All the expellees and "refugees" together may be divided into two main categories, the *Volksdeutsche* and the *Reichsdeutsche*. The former, often called the ethnic Germans, included more than 2.5 million persons of German descent who had been citizens of countries in which their families had long resided. Some of them, notably in the Sudetenland, had conspired with the Nazis and were among the beneficiaries of Hitler's aggression. Following the collapse of the Third Reich, the Czechoslovak government was the first to deprive its German population of citizenship and to order its expulsion, a course subsequently followed by other Eastern European regimes. The *Reichsdeutsche* included about 10 million persons with German citizenship who lived in the areas taken by Poland—Pomerania, Silesia, East Brandenburg, East Prussia and Danzig. The ruthless expulsion of Germans constituted one of the largest mass deportations in history.

The infiltrees or interzonal refugees are Germans who moved —usually illegally—from one zone of occupation to another. More than a million infiltrees are now living illegally in the Western zones, while as many as 30,000 a month continue to cross over from Eastern Germany. The evacuees are persons who were evicted from their residences in Germany during military operations. Although many of them returned to their homes after the war, in January 1948 almost 4 million were still dislodged.

The fourth layer of refugees in Europe consists of non-Germans escaping from the Soviet Union and Eastern Europe. During the summer of 1946, 120,000 Jews fled from Poland following new pogroms, and 7,000 Czechoslovaks left their country immediately after the coup d'état of February 1948. A steady influx has since been entering Austria and Western Germany, estimates of the monthly rate varying between 600 and 4,000. From Poland, Czechoslovakia and Hungary approximately 150,000 had crossed the border by June 1, 1950. Over 2,000 Iron Curtain refugees were living in the Trieste Territory. The latest movement consists of some 250,000 Bulgarian Turks threatened with deportation to Turkey, of whom 30,000 had crossed the line by September 1950.

In Greece about 250,000 persons were evacuated during World War II. The number of Greek refugees because of the civil war reached a peak of almost one million in May 1949, but with the termination of hostilities, virtually complete resettlement is expected. . . . In addition to these major categories, odd groups of refugees are scattered in many parts of the world, stray remnants of ancient communities like the Assyrians in Iraq who are still looking for permanent homes and the soldiers of General Anders' Polish army which fought in Italy, 150,000 of whom—including dependents—have found temporary haven in Britain. The story of the world's refugees is a tragic revelation of man's callous disregard for human rights. . . .

COMPASSION BY SLIDE RULE [4]

Seldom has there been a more calculated piece of legislative hypocrisy than the Refugee Relief Act of 1953. Though thousands of "wetbacks" cross the Mexican border into the United States every year without benefit of passport, Congress has made legal immigration by European refugees from communism all but impossible.

If you wanted to bring a refugee family from Europe to live in your home, to work on your farm, to teach in your school —or for any other reason of selfishness or altruism that might occur to you—the probability is that you couldn't do it. The refugee law ("a great humanitarian act," President Eisenhower called it) stands squarely in your way to keep the refugees where they are—or in any event, away from the United States.

Ostensibly, the act lays out the welcome mat for over 200,000 victims of Nazi and Communist oppression—chiefly political refugees and "escapees" from behind the Iron Curtain—over a three-year period ending in 1956. But in the name of "security" it has been cluttered up with so many restrictions and prohibitions that it is virtually inoperable. At the beginning of [1955], with almost a third of the period gone, some five hundred refugees had cleared the mountainous hurdles set for them and reached these shores. If, under existing circumstances, as many as ten thousand make it before the act expires, it will be little short of miraculous.

The President had great hopes for the bill when he signed it into law in August 1953. "It demonstrates again," he said pridefully, "America's concern for the homeless, the persecuted, and the less fortunate of other lands." That sentiment was shared by millions in the United States and around the world. In the bleak, jammed refugee centers of Western Europe where hope is like a dimly remembered dream, it brought a fresh vision of deliverance. But that was before the booby traps were sprung.

[4] From "That Phony Refugee Law," by Cabell Phillips of the New York *Times* Washington bureau. *Harper's Magazine.* 210:68-72. April 1955. Reprinted by permission.

Pressure to put some justice and workability in the refugee act has been mounting . . . for the cost of this fakery has been high. First, hordes of democratically-minded Europeans, who gambled their lives and their livelihood on the West's promise of freedom if they fled their oppressors, now find those promises empty. Second, thousands of Americans sincerely wanting to help provide a haven for these uprooted millions are frustrated in their desire. And third, we have made a mockery before the rest of the world—and particularly before our propaganda-wise Communist enemies—of those sentiments of compassion, generosity, and humanitarianism which we proclaim so proudly.

If you as a citizen well disposed toward your fellow man, should decide that you wanted to sponsor the relocation of a refugee family in this country—it might be a kinsman, a professional colleague, a promising scholar, or just an anonymous "case" whom you would like to see get a fair shake out of life— you would find the responsibility so onerous that you probably would want to back out of it.

First, you would be required to execute a binding agreement with the government that you, personally, guarantee that the alien and his family will not become public charges. You buttress this with affidavits about your own employment and income, your bank credit, and a copy of your last income-tax return. Your church, your service club, or some local welfare agency cannot share this responsibility with you; it is yours alone.

Second, you cannot defer getting your alien a job until after he arrives and has had a chance to look around. You must fill out a form at the start specifying that you have procured for him a particular job with a named employer at a stated wage which does not displace any other job holder. All this must be certified by the local representative of the United States Employment Service and then by the Department of Labor in Washington. It is up to you to see that the job is held open until your alien arrives, which is calculated—even under "normal" circumstances, which do not now exist—at anywhere from four to eight months.

Third, you must be equally explicit about the housing you have provided—the street address, a description of the accommodations, the name and address of the landlord.

After at least a couple of months—and probably a good amount of anguished reappraisal—you may have assembled all of your documents and mailed them off to the Refugee Relief Administrator, at the Department of State, in Washington. Then the wheels of bureaucracy will slowly begin to grind on the other side of the ocean. Your alien naturally will have to go through a mass of red tape to qualify himself to emigrate. But two hurdles will be unique, and quite possibly, insurmountable.

First, he must procure from some government—preferably the one under which he is currently living—a guarantee that they will readmit him if at any time and under any circumstances his residence in the United States is terminated. The groundwork for these guarantees has been concluded with most countries by diplomatic negotiation during the last year. But each guarantee is issued individually on the merits of the particular case, which creates frightening complications for most refugees. Their welcome has already worn thin in most instances—West Germany has absorbed over seven million into her fragile economy—and their hosts are understandably reluctant to take them back once they have departed.

Second, your alien must affirmatively establish his political and ideological purity of heart for at least two years preceding his application to emigrate. In other words, he must pass a security check of his neighbors, fellow workers, employers, and the police to show that he is free of Communist or other subversive taint. This is a manifest impossibility in most cases since the neighbors, friends, and police records are somewhere on the other side of the Iron Curtain, where even the FBI doesn't venture to go. Some refugees who have lived long enough in the West and have come favorably under the eye of our counter-intelligence corps have become eligible for security clearance. But for the majority, there is nothing for them to do but wait out their two years' probation in a state of such exemplary grace as to prove to the most skeptical that they just couldn't be Communists.

As an individual sponsor, then, you would have a very tough time of it, indeed. You would find—like thousands of other well-meaning citizens—that the humanitarian concepts of the refugee bill have been all but washed out by the slide-rule techniques for administering it. But if you still persisted, you would be well advised to turn your problem over to one of the dozen organizations constituting the American Council of Voluntary Agencies for Foreign Service, Inc. They cannot wholly relieve you of your personal responsibility and they cannot by-pass the legal hurdles—but they can put up a better fight than you can against legislative and bureaucratic obstinacy.

"I have been working in the field of immigration since 1939, and under every statute we have had dealing with refugees," says Miss Ann Petluck of the United HIAS [Hebrew Immigrant Aid Society] Service, an agency dealing principally with the problems of Jewish resettlement. "I have never run into as many road-blocks as I have under this 1953 act.

"The key to the difficulty is simply this: Congress couldn't make up its mind whether it wanted humanitarian legislation, a means of importing cheap labor, or neither. Out of that sort of confusion nothing but stalemate could come, and that is what we have."

The legislative history of the act bears out this contention. Since World War II we have financed to the tune of billions of dollars the restoration of the broken societies of Europe and Asia. We have led in the work of such humane ventures as UNRRA and the International Relief Organization which have been primarily concerned with the millions of uprooted, homeless, and destitute victims of, first, Fascist, and later, Communist conquest. Living meagerly in refugee camps or in the crowded slums of Germany, Austria, Italy, and Greece, these hopeless masses are not only a challenge to the humanitarian instincts of civilized people everywhere, but also a deadly burden on the struggling economies of the host governments.

There is no solution to this refugee problem but resettlement, and many governments are sharing the burden. Canada has taken more than 800,000, Australia 700,000, Argentina 500,000, and Brazil 200,000. Under the Displaced Persons Act, the United States absorbed over 400,000 between 1948 and 1952. But there are still some six to eight million refugees without homes or means of support in Western Europe—many of them lured there by our own propaganda. In effect, we promised them "liberation," and they stole by the thousands through the barbed wire and across the mine fields that are the true Iron Curtain.

The DP Act expired at about the time the Immigration and Nationality Act of 1952—the McCarran-Walter Act—went into effect. This was the first major revision of our basic immigration code in more than two decades, and it was the most restrictive ever to go on the statute books. Not only did it make no provisions for refugees, as such; it impeded what had been the normal flow of regular immigration. President Truman vetoed it unsuccessfully, but he never ceased condemning it. In the presidential campaign of 1952, both General Eisenhower and Governor Stevenson promised repeatedly that if elected they would demand extensive revisions in the McCarran-Walter Act. And as President, Mr. Eisenhower reiterated his promise in his State of the Union message of 1953, and in April specifically requested such legislation in letters to the Vice President and the Speaker of the House. And there the funny business began.

Standing out fiercely against any kind of tampering with his great legislative monument was that florid and irascible old xenophobe, the late Senator Pat McCarran, of Nevada. Aligned with him were Representative Francis E. Walter, of Pennsylvania, co-author of the bill, and a coterie of about a score of senators and representatives who can always be counted upon to spring noisily to arms whenever a "mongrel" invasion from across the seas threatens. This is a powerful bloc, and it was clear to Republican leaders, particularly in the Senate, that efforts to get such a revision would provoke a bitter and probably a losing fight.

They laid this dilemma before the President, it now appears, and urged that if he would forgo his insistence on softening the McCarran-Walter Act they would undertake to get, in exchange, some sort of special legislation for refugees. This, at least, they argued, would quiet the minority groups who were doing all the shouting. The President apparently agreed to this substitution in good faith; he probably did not know he was swapping something for nothing. At all events nothing more was heard about revising the McCarran-Walter Act and in due course hearings were begun on a refugee bill.

There is no surer means of whipping up the fears and prejudices of the uninformed than to create the bogy that a lot of foreigners are about to do us out of something. Horns and serpent's teeth may be added to the apparition by draping the red cloak of communism about it. This is precisely the atmosphere in which the Refugee Act of 1953 took shape. Guidance was provided by Representative Walter in the House, and in the Senate by Senators McCarran, Welker of Idaho, Jenner of Indiana, Butler of Maryland, and Eastland of Mississippi.

Spokesmen for the Administration and for church, welfare, labor, and nationality groups supported a generous measure based on experience gained under the Displaced Persons Act. They advocated the admission of 240,000 refugees over a two-year period, with no substantial tightening of the screening and security proceedures that had formerly been used. This additional number of refugees, they argued, would put no measurable burden on the economy nor threaten the job opportunities of native-born citizens. Not more than a fraction of 1 per cent of former refugees had become public charges, and none had been formally charged with engaging in subversive activities. To sabotage the program by excessive restrictions and security safeguards, they contended, not only would be pointless but would defeat its whole humanitarian goal.

The futility of the policeman's approach to the problem was succinctly put by the Reverend Basil A. Malof, president of the Russian Bible Society and a one-time refugee himself. Asked by Senator Welker if it were not conceivable that the Soviets were covertly fostering the flight of refugees across their borders and freely infiltrating them with spies, he replied:

No, sir. That has never happened and can never happen as long as Communists are Communists. . . . They don't need to do it, because they can get as many people across the Mexican border as they want to without passports, and across the Canadian border if they want to. These escapees are, I would say, 90 per cent genuine people who will expose communism, which is necessary in this country to be done.

All such testimony was politely listened to. But what most excited the interrogators, what gave them texts for elaborate exhortations of their own, were the grim and strident prophesies of disaster that came from the organized anti-foreign, super-American forces of the far Right.

George Racey Jordan, speaking for the American Coalition of American Patriotic Societies, told the Senate Judiciary subcommittee:

Congress should not yield to sentimentality for aliens abroad but should put the welfare of the people of the United States first and foremost. I tell you, they [refugees] will wind up in the big industrial cities, and on relief, and taking jobs away from our soldiers who are going to come home from Korea one of these days.

And Mrs. James C. Lucas, of the Daughters of the American Revolution, saw the whole thing as a part of a gigantic spy plot.

What a golden opportunity [she cried to the committee] for these Communist-dominated countries to plant subversives under the guise of "expellees" with the definite aim to enter and undermine our Republic. There are already between three and five million illegal aliens roaming around these United States.

Representative Walter dourly told the House when the bill was presented on the floor there: "I do not think these people are the kind of people our ancestors were." And Senator Jenner angrily posed and answered this rhetorical question to his colleagues in the Upper Chamber:

We have given $40 billion to help people all over the world because we are told communism thrives on hunger. Yet, in the last few days we have seen the people of Germany become so hungry that they were willing to fight the Communists with their bare fists. What do we now propose to do? We propose to feed them so that they will not fight communism any more.

The real fight came on the Senate's version of the bill. McCarran and Jenner joined forces in the Judiciary subcommittee hearings to force into the text virtually every restrictive and crippling device that had been proposed. They lifted from the McCarran-Walter Act the hotly controversial "national origins" theory as the basis for quota determinations. They weakened the bill's central purpose—the aid of European refugees—by making it applicable to countries where the refugee problem is virtually non-existent. They reduced the number to be aided from 240,000 to 209,000 and lengthened the time span from two years to three. Against the advice of State Department and immigration authorities, they insisted upon the two-year security check and the readmission proviso. They blocked group sponsorship of refugees by agencies, to put the burden on individual citizens; and they denied former refugees the right to act as sponsors. And then, to take care of anything they might have overlooked, they demanded that administration of the act be put in the "safe" hands of Scott McLeod, the security chief of the Department of State, instead of under the separate new bureau which the sponsors had proposed.

Finally, to shield their grotesque creation from assault, they held the bill off the Senate floor until the last, crowded week of the session and threatened to filibuster any substantive amendments offered from the floor. Their stratagem worked. The bill passed 62 to 30; the President was given a bill "for the relief of refugees," but the anti-refugee forces yielded scarcely a foot of ground. Senator Herbert Lehman, of New York, epitomized the sense of frustration and despair with which many voted reluctantly for the bill when he said:

> There are many provisions of this bill which I would oppose with all my strength if the legislative situation were different from what it actually is. I believe that provisions of this bill are so onerous and impossible of reasonable enforcement that great difficulties will be encountered and many individuals who should be admitted will be denied admission. . . . But I would not wish to assume the responsibility for delaying a final vote on this measure, which must be passed before the session ends.

Inevitably, relief under the refugee act has materialized at a snail's pace. The latest figures released by Mr. McLeod's office show that visas have at last been issued for a total of 18,936 persons, but of these 570 were orphans and only 563 were refugees and escapees. [For later figures see "The New Broom," in this section, below.] All the rest were special category immigrants who bear little or no relation to the refugee problem. There is meanwhile a backlog of about 23,000 assurances from sponsors. Viewed in terms of willingness to undertake the onerous responsibilities of bringing a refugee family to this country, that is a pretty impressive figure. But set against the target of

209,000 refugees to be admitted by the end of 1956 it is a shocking indictment of the capricious spirit in which the refugee act was written. . . .

There is really nothing wrong with this act that can't be corrected if the task is approached with honesty and sincerity [a church official prominent in refugee affairs said recently]. I believe if the President insists on substance as well as on form in refugee legislation, it can be amended to do the job he intended it to do.

But we can't reach that goal if every refugee is to be regarded, per se, as a Communist, a chiseler, and a competitor for some American boy's job. After all, there's a bit of the refugee in every American's bloodstream. It doesn't become us very well to try to dodge that fact.

But despite all counsels of moderation, humanity, and good sense, the Refugee Relief Act still stands in the books as a national disgrace.

THE CORSI IMBROGLIO [5]

[Secretary of State John Foster] Dulles introduced burly, bald Ed Corsi to Washington newsmen on December 30 [1954] as an "old friend" and newly chosen consultant, summoned from New York to help speed up immigration under the 1953 Refugee Relief Act. Dulles labeled him "the best qualified man in the United States" for the job: Corsi came to the United States as an immigrant lad himself, rose to become United States Commissioner of Immigration, served as New York Industrial Commissioner, ran unsuccessfully as Republican candidate for mayor of New York and United States Senator.

In passing the Refugee Relief Act, Congress had specifically assigned its administration to the State Department's Security Director, Scott McLeod. Corsi, however, felt that his position should rank McLeod; he wanted to be named special assistant to the Secretary of State. While he was on a European tour, checking up on the refugee program, he was given the title in a cable from Dulles.

[5] From "90-Day Wonder." *Time.* 65:19. April 25, 1955. Reprinted by permission.

Corsi planned to recruit ten thousand refugee German farmers for field labor in California, in place of Mexican wetbacks. He hoped to bring in a shipload of a thousand immigrant Italian cooks and bakers, and maybe a shipload of tailors, too, to come steaming up the Hudson in time for a July Fourth picnic. He wanted to short-cut the act's delaying provisions, which require advance guarantees of jobs and housing for refugees. Unfortunately, some of his plans collided with the law as written by Congress; moreover, he initially refused to take his place as McLeod's deputy in charge of the refugee program.

On March 16 McLeod offered Corsi two choices: (1) become deputy, or (2) retire "gracefully and with dignity" by taking a special temporary job surveying immigration in South America. Corsi hesitated. He felt, McLeod said, that "the title [deputy] didn't have a very good ring to it." Furthermore, as Corsi said later, he was "ashamed" of his "rat hole in the wall" State Department office. Meanwhile, Pennsylvania's Democratic Congressman Francis Walter attacked Corsi on the ground that he had once belonged to some Communist front groups. At his news conference on April 5, Dulles disclosed publicly for the first time that Corsi's job had only a ninety-day tenure. Understandably, the press jumped to the conclusion that Congressman Walter's attack had prompted Dulles to fire Corsi. It kept jumping as Dulles and other Administration sources, on and off the record, made one bumbling explanation after another of the Corsi case.

Last week the ninety days were up and Corsi quit, with a letter to Secretary Dulles denouncing "an intolerant minority, both in Congress and within the State Department itself, which believes that in this world there are superior and inferior races. These people are sabotaging the refugee program and have brought about my elimination." . . .

North Dakota's Republican Senator William Langer began an investigation. He summoned before his Senate Immigration subcommittee, as its first witness, the State Department's McLeod, who defended his administration of the refugee program. His report: 24,810 immigrant visas issued so far, and another 75,587 being processed out of 214,000 permitted by the act, with twenty months still to go.

As for Corsi, McLeod said unhappily: "I could never tie Mr. Corsi 'down as to what he was doing, or I was doing, or who was running the program."

THE NEW BROOM [6]

An urgent assignment to speed up the lagging refugee immigration program was handed today to Pierce J. Gerety, forty-one-year-old New York and Connecticut lawyer.

He took up the new and politically controversial post with the public blessing of President Eisenhower and John Foster Dulles, Secretary of State.

Technically, Mr. Gerety's title is Deputy Administrator of the Refugee Program. But his superior, Scott McLeod, who accompanied him to the White House, said that he had delegated to Mr. Gerety complete policy and operational authority.

The program is designed to bring into this country by the end of next year 209,000 refugees and relatives of immigrants already in the United States.

Mr. Gerety . . . takes on an assignment similar to that from which Edward J. Corsi of New York was ousted recently. Mr. Corsi was a special assistant to Secretary Dulles on refugee problems.

Mr. Corsi made no secret of his distaste for Mr. McLeod and what he called the "security gang." He said that they had imposed unnecessary restrictions on the entry of refugees. Mr. Corsi was abruptly notified that his employment was ended after ninety days.

It was made clear that there was no time limit on Mr. Gerety's employment. He said that he was "happy" to serve

[6] From a dispatch to the New York *Times* from W. H. Lawrence of the *Times* Washington bureau. New York *Times.* p 1+. June 10, 1955. Reprinted by permission.

under Mr. McLeod, who has been a target for sharp criticism on and off Capitol Hill.

The announcement of Mr. Gerety's appointment was made at the State Department. He was taken at once to the White House for a conference with the President, Mr. Dulles and Mr. McLeod.

"The President told me that he wished to see the program succeed, and I assured him that I am determined to make it succeed," Mr. Gerety, a calm and soft-spoken man, said after the picture-taking ceremony had ended. . . .

Mr. Gerety will not go to work at the State Department for a few days. However, one of his first actions, after the appointment was announced, was to call on Representative Francis E. Walter, Democrat of Pennsylvania, and co-author of the McCarran-Walter Immigration Act.

Mr. Corsi and Mr. Walter had engaged in a sharp dispute.

Mr. Walter said after the forty-five-minute meeting that he had been "well pleased with Mr. Gerety's interest in the real refugee problem." . . .

High political stakes conceivably could ride on the success of Mr. Gerety's efforts. The position of the Administration with minority groups has not been helped by the criticism of Mr. Corsi, who called the refugee program "a complete failure and a national scandal." He has been influential particularly among Americans of Italian descent.

The program was authorized in August 1953, and as of June 3, visas had been issued for 32,842 persons. Of these, 9,140 were classified as refugees, 1,106 as orphans and 22,596 as relatives of persons already living in this country.

By May 27, the Immigration Service reported that 22,301 persons actually had been admitted, of which 3,724 were classified as refugees, 750 as orphans and 17,827 as relatives.

There was on June 3 a backlog of 84,645 visa applications being processed in all parts of the world.

Visas have been authorized at a rate in excess of 1,200 a week recently. Mr. McLeod said that the ratio of refugees to other entrants was "catching up."

CHANGES WOULD IMPERIL SECURITY [7]

The agitation in behalf of the so-called Refugee Act, precipitated by President Eisenhower's request for still greater leniencies, unmasks the Act for what it is: a fraudulent gesture of political hypocrisy.

For all its purported humanitarian aims, the Act is a crudely-concocted piece of old-fashioned pork-barreling on an international level. By itself and in combination with the proposals for revision it represents a clear and dangerous attempt to circumvent the carefully constructed legislation which now stands as this nation's basic policy on immigration.

The people of the United States were duped when they were told of its need. The fact is that during the past three years, immigration pressures from the outside have continuously diminished, and the conditions upon which the displaced persons laws of 1948 and 1950 were predicated have all but disappeared.

A recently released State Department report states bluntly that despite the broadest interpretations as to qualifications, there are not enough applicants to use up even the visas provided for originally in the Refugee Act—a total of 209,000. There is no mass of starving, tortured humanity pounding at our doors.

Let me cite a few excerpts from the State Department report issued by the administrator of the refugee program, Scott McLeod:

In Germany, he reports: "East German escapees, constituting the largest single bloc of potentially qualified aliens in West Germany, have the same working rights as West Germans. Greatly improved economic conditions in Germany will reduce the demand for visas under the act as many refugees are being integrated into the local economy."

Not only the regular immigration quota for people born in Germany—which is 25,000 a year—is open and visas are cur-

[8] By Representative Francis E. Walter (Democrat, Pennsylvania), chairman of the House Un-American Activities Committee, chairman of the Subcommittee on Immigration, and co-author of the Immigration and Nationality Act of 1952. New York *Journal-American*. p 19. July 27, 1955. Reprinted by permission. This is the first part of a pro-and-con discussion of the Refugee Relief Act of 1953. The second, by Senator Herbert H. Lehman, follows.

rently available, but preference portions of every immigration quota for Eastern European countries are open just as well.

Of the 2,000 visas allocated for Polish refugees residing in England, only 250 have been applied for.

In the Netherlands "the initiative shown by the Dutch government in repairing the flood damage and in caring for the inhabitants of the flood areas, plus full employment, make it difficult for applicants to qualify as refugees."

The improved conditions that have enabled these peoples to become adjusted and integrated should be a source of tremendous pride to the American people. This has come about almost wholly as a result of the $38 billion which we have provided, in a genuine humanitarian endeavor, to promote recovery abroad.

The Senate and House conferees on the refugee bill, at the time of its enactment, stressed that it was not to be considered a "mandate to issue the full number of visas. . . . These are maximum limitations, not quotas to be filled." But instead of taking satisfaction in the fact that the crisis has ended, the sponsors of the new recommendations are expressing great concern now that the "goal" of 209,000 additional immigrants may not be met. The Refugee Act as a consequence is being transformed into a grotesque Cinderella's shoe.

To justify the changes, the President explained that a "number of the provisions of the act require amendment if the act's objectives are to be fully met."

Let us examine some of the proposed changes and see how they would destroy even the limited safeguards of the original law.

The Act of 1953 established a genuine hardship test for qualification as a refugee and requires that the prospective immigrant is not firmly resettled and is "in urgent need of assistance for the essentials of life." It clearly did not wish to provide a "better bet" for persons who merely felt they could improve their lot in the Eldorado of America. The amendment proposals would upset this test completely.

Under the Act of 1953, provisions for immigrant status, with the subsequent privilege of becoming citizens, were extended to five thousand alien residents who lawfully entered the United

States before July 1, 1953, and who cannot return to their homelands because of the peril of persecution. The demand that they had entered the country legally would seem a small enough one in exchange for the privilege conferred upon them. The amendment bills, however, would eliminate this requirement and bestow this privilege on *any* alien, including the ship jumpers and those who have simply sneaked across the border.

Closely allied to this is another proposal to eliminate the present requirement for complete information regarding the two years immediately preceding the application for entry of each prospective immigrant. Such a change would strike at the heart of our security system. Refugee camps in Germany are permeated with Communist agents ordered by the Soviets to adopt new undercover lives in Europe and America to carry out underground activities. Only the most careful scrutiny of past records can bring about the detection of these agents. Eliminating this provision in the 1953 Act would prove of inestimable aid to Communist infiltration tactics which we have now begun to combat with increasing success.

When I was in Berlin recently, the chief of the United States Counter-Intelligence Corps, entrusted with the responsibility for the security investigations under the Refugee Act, was appalled at suggestions that the two-year requirement be dropped. He recommended instead that it be extended to five years.

The Act of 1953 specified that each prospective immigrant be sponsored by a responsible citizen, or citizens, who would guarantee that the new arrival would not displace someone else from a job or home. The obligation would rest solely upon the sponsors. Interestingly enough, there has been a notable lack of such sponsors. In the new proposals, sponsorship could be undertaken by "approved" organizations. In the case of public or semi-public agencies, the immigrant would automatically become a "public charge," a situation which immigration laws throughout our history have been designed to prevent.

Another measure includes the presidential recommendation to suspend the health requirements of our immigration laws to permit the entry of persons afflicted by tuberculosis, one of Europe's most rampant diseases. "We in the United States no longer regard tuberculosis with dread," the President declared. The United States Public Health Service lists it as one of the nation's most fearsome killers, with an annual death toll of around 25,000. We have been battling this scourge with tremendous expenditures of money and medical talent. It has cost us untold wealth in the form of men and women lost to productive labor through its ravages. Are we now to import it deliberately?

The welfare of this nation, in regard to augmenting our population from outside sources, is, I believe, best served by the diligently-constructed [McCarran-Walter] Immigration Law. . . . This law provides the best coordination of our responsibility to ourselves as a nation and of our responsibility to the rest of the world. It permits us to remain of the same fibre that proved over the last stormy half century too tough to be subverted or conquered by any brand of totalitarianism.

The enactment of that law stands as an accomplishment which should not be subjected to partisan and demagogic ventures which can result only in the defeat of our purposes both here and abroad.

REFUGEE RELIEF PROGRAM A DREARY FAILURE [8]

For almost ten years now the Voice of America has been exhorting freedom-loving people from behind the Iron Curtain to escape to freedom. We have been describing the glories and advantages of the free world. We have been extolling the blessings of liberty and justice.

But how do we treat those who flee from Soviet tyranny and Communist brutality? Ask those who have been to Europe and have visited the refugee camps in Austria, Western Germany and Italy. Hear their descriptions of the barbed wire entanglements, the cells, hovels and barracks where hundreds and thousands of men, women and children live lives of savage desperation.

[7] By Senator Herbert H. Lehman (Democrat, New York), author of an omnibus bill to repeal the McCarran-Walter Act and liberalize immigration policy. New York *Journal-American*. p 18. July 28, 1955. Reprinted by permission.

The refugees from war and postwar upheaval and the escapees from behind the Iron Curtain find a cold hospitality in the facilities set aside for them. Some, it is true, have found jobs and have established new lives in one or another of the countries of Western Europe, in Australia, Canada and South America. Some few have come to the United States.

But as far as the United States is concerned, the number of refugees and escapees who have been admitted here are precious few, indeed.

More than half the life span of the Refugee Relief program is over. But only about one tenth of the number authorized to be admitted have actually been permitted to come to the United States.

The refugee program has been a failure. It has been a source of disappointment and disillusionment to thousands of people abroad. The failure of this program—the way in which it has operated—has exposed our country to ridicule and resentment abroad. It has been an open scandal. Why?

A major cause has been the cruel and heartless way in which the program has until very recently been administered. The red tape was endless. The investigations were interminable. The questionnaires which the applicants had to fill out were voluminous, complex and treacherous. The attitude of our officials, both abroad and in Washington, was cold and unsympathetic.

It is true that in recent months the Administration has "softened" its attiude toward the refugees. President Eisenhower, very belatedly, issued instructions to expedite the program. There seems to have been lately a genuine effort to make the program work.

It must also be said, however, that the conversion has been rather tardy, coming after public exposure of the program's failure. A number of us in Congress have been critical of the Administration since the spring of 1954. Then, of course, came the Corsi affair [see "The Corsi Imbroglio," in this section above] and the country stood up and took notice. So did the Administration.

Despite the belated change in Administration attitude, however, the program is still critically handicapped by the provisions of the law itself. The Refugee Relief Act, as passed in 1953, contained so many restrictions and booby-traps, that entry into the United States under the refugee program became a challenge which relatively few could meet.

On May 27, 1955—two years later—President Eisenhower finally recognized the defects in the Refugee Relief Act and officially recommended to Congress a series of amendments. Some weeks before the President made his proposals, I had submitted a somewhat more comprehensive set of amendments, although I frankly admit that there were some points in the President's proposals which I had not covered in mine and which certainly merit favorable action by Congress. . . .

It is essential that whatever bill is enacted include provisions to enable the admission of the full authorized number of refugees and escapees—if not by December 1956, then by some later date. The United States must open its gates to this relatively small number of refugees and escapees.

Other major provisions which ought to be included in any bill of amendments to the Refugee Act might be summarized as follows:

(1) Eliminate the infamous "two-year history" requirement —the requirement that each escapee furnish a documented record of his two previous years of activity—an impossibility for most recent escapees;

(2) Eliminate the prohibition against so-called agency assurances—assurances by the great religious and non-sectarian voluntary agencies that they will be responsible for the individual refugees they sponsor for admission;

(3) Simplify the now unworkable definitions of "escapee," "refugee," and "expellee."

(4) Make the Administrator of the program directly responsible to the Secretary of State, and make clear that Congress means the refugee program to be implemented and not frustrated.

(5) Eliminate the requirement that after the consular officer decides an applicant is eligible, under the terms of the Refugee Act, an immigration officer may separately sit in judgment on the same facts.

(6) Raise the maximum age of orphans who may be brought over for adoption, under the program, from ten to fourteen years of age.

(7) Eliminate the requirement that each applicant have a valid passport from his country of origin or residence—an impossibility for many escapees and refugees from Communist tyranny.

(8) Eliminate the requirement that each applicant must have a certificate from his country of present residence, guaranteeing readmission to that country, if at any time in the future, and for any reason, the United States should decide to deport him.

Above all, it is necessary that the Congress and the Administration show a clear appreciation of the high importance—in terms of our foreign policy, our humanitarian principles, and our own national origin and traditions—of serving as an example, before the world, of hospitality and haven for the oppressed and persecuted.

We should all remember, however, that the Refugee Relief Act is only a temporary emergency program. Every refugee or relative coming to our country under the Refugee Act must also qualify for admission under the stringent and harsh provisions of our basic immigration and naturalization laws. We must not forget that the revision of the refugee program is only a small skirmish in the over-all struggle to provide the United States with a permanent, reasonable and humanitarian immigration program.

[For a discussion of the omnibus immigration and naturalization bill sponsored by Senator Lehman, see "Time for a Change?" in this section, above.]

BIBLIOGRAPHY

An asterisk (*) preceding a reference indicates that the article or a part of it has been reprinted in this book.

BOOKS AND PAMPHLETS

Abbott, Edith. Historical aspects of the immigration problem: select documents. 881p. University of Chicago Press. Chicago. '26.

Adamic, Louis. From many lands. 350p. Harper & Bros. New York. '40.

Adamic, Louis. Plymouth Rock and Ellis Island. 16p. Common Council for American Unity. 20 W. 40th St. New York 18. '40.

Adamic, Louis. What's your name? 248p. Harper & Bros. New York. '42.

Adamic, Louis and Addes, G. F. Foreign born Americans and the war. 22p. American Committee for the Protection of the Foreign Born, 23 E. 26th St. New York 10. '43.

Adamic, Louis. Nation of nations. 399p. Harper & Bros. New York. '45.

American Committee for Protection of Foreign Born. Walter-McCarran law—extracts from testimony before President's commission on immigration and naturalization. 36p. The Committee. 23 W. 26th St. New York 10. '53.

American Friends Service Committee. If this be liberty. 20p. The Committee. 20 S. 12th St. Philadelphia 7. '53.

American Jewish Committee. Fact sheet on the McCarran immigration act. 7p. The Committee. 386 4th Ave. New York 16. '53.

American Jewish Committee. The Lehman immigration and naturalization bill—a summary. 4p. The Committee. 386 4th Ave. New York 16. '53.

American Jewish Committee. "Whom we shall welcome"—a summary of the report of the President's commission on immigration and naturalization. 7p. The Committee. 386 4th Ave. New York 16. '53.

American Jewish Congress. Commission on Law and Social Action Reports. Analysis of Refugee Relief Act of 1953. 6p. The Congress. 15 E. 84th St. New York 28. '53.

American Jewish Congress. Commission on Law and Social Action Reports. The Refugee Relief Act of 1953—paper victory? 9p. The Congress. 15 E. 84th St. New York 28. '53.

Anti-Defamation League of B'nai B'rith. Refugee Relief Act of 1953—a commentary. 9p. The League. 212 5th Ave. New York 10. '53.

Auerbach, F. L. Admission and resettlement of displaced persons in the United States. 56p. Common Council for American Unity. 20 W. 40th St. New York 18. '50.

Auerbach, F. L. Immigration and Nationality Act; a summary of its principal provisions. 103p. Common Council for American Unity. 20 W. 40th St. New York 18. '52.

Auerbach, F. L. Immigration laws of the United States. 372p. Bobbs-Merrill Co. Indianapolis, Ind. '55.

Blegen, T. C. ed. Land of their choice; the immigrants write home. 463p. University of Minnesota Press. Minneapolis. '55.

Brown, F. J. and Roucek, J. S. eds. One America: the history, contributions, and present problems of our racial and national minorities. 764p. Prentice Hall. New York. '52.

Bruce, J. C. Golden door; the irony of our immigration policy. 244p. Random House. New York. '54.

Bernard, W. S. ed. American immigration policy, a reappraisal. 341p. Harper & Bros. New York. '50.

Bogardus, E. S. Immigration and race attitudes. 294p. D. C. Heath & Co. Boston. '28.

Bowers, D. F. ed. Foreign influences in American life. 254p. Princeton University Press. Princeton, N.J. '44.

Buaken, Manuel. I have lived with the American people. 358p. Caxton Printers. Caldwell, Idaho. '48.

Center for Information on America. Immigration, "whom shall we welcome?" (Vital Issues Discussion Guide. v2, no9) 4p. The Center. Washington, Conn. '53.

*Cohen, F. S. Immigration and national welfare. 40p. League for Industrial Democracy. 112 E. 19th St. New York 3. '40.

Committee to Improve U. S. Immigration Law. United States immigration policy; statement of position by major religious, labor, civic, and nationality groups. 40p. The Committee. 60 E. 42d St. New York 17. '52.

Common Council for American Unity. European beliefs regarding the United States. 140p. The Council. 20 W. 40th St. New York 18. '49.

Cooley, O. W. and Poirot, Paul. Freedom to move. 34p. Foundation for Economic Education. Irvington-on-Hudson. New York. '51.

Coon, C. S., Garn, S. M., and Birdsell, J. B. Races: a study of the problems of race formation in man. (American Lecture Series no77) 153p. C. C. Thomas. Springfield, Ill. '50.

*Corsi, Edward. Paths to the new world; American immigration—yesterday, today, and tomorrow. (Freedom Pamphlet Series) 46p. Anti-Defamation League of B'nai B'rith. 212 5th Ave. New York 10. '53.

Davie, M. R. World immigration. 588p. Macmillan. New York. '36.

Davie, M. R. and others. Refugees in America. 453p. Harper & Bros. New York. '47.

Dominion of Canada. Department of Citizenship and Immigration. Immigration procedure for those settling in Canada. 12p. Edmond Cloutier, Queen's Printer and Controller of Stationery. Ottawa, Canada. '54.

Duncan, H. G. Immigration and assimilation. 890p. D. C. Heath & C. Boston. '33.

Eaton, A. H. Immigrant gifts to American life. 185p. Russell Sage Foundation. New York. '32.

Forsyth, W. D. Myth of open spaces. 226p. Melbourne University Press. Melbourne, Australia. '42.

Fairchild, H. P. Immigration. 520p. Macmillan. New York. '45.

Fairchild, H. P. Race and nationality are factors in American life. 216p. Ronald Press. New York. '47.

Fields, Harold. Refugee in the United States. 229p. Oxford University Press. New York. '38.

Gibson, W. M. Aliens and the law. 200p. University of North Carolina Press. Chapel Hill, N.C. '40.

Grant, Madison and Davidson, C. S. eds. Aliens in our midst. 238p. Galton Publishing Co. New York. '30.

Green, Abner. Walter-McCarran law, police state terror against foreign-born Americans. 48p. American Committee for Protection of Foreign Born. 23 W. 26th St. New York 10. '53.

Green, Abner. In the shadow of liberty. 48p. American Committee for Protection of Foreign Born. 23 W. 26th St. New York 10. '54.

Guillet, E. C. Great migration. 284p. Thomas Nelson & Sons. New York. '37.

Handlin, Oscar. This was America. 602p. Harvard University Press. Cambridge, Mass. '49.

Handlin, Oscar. Uprooted; the epic story of the great migrations that made the American people. 310p. Little, Brown Co. Boston. '51.

Handlin, Oscar. Adventures in freedom: three hundred years of Jewish life in America. 282p. McGraw-Hill. New York. '54.

Handlin, Oscar. American people in the twentieth century. 244p. Harvard University Press. Cambridge, Mass. '54.

Hansen, M. L. Atlantic migration, 1607-1860. 391p. Harvard University Press. Cambridge, Mass. '40.

Hansen, M. L. Immigrant in American history. 230p. Harvard University Press. Cambridge, Mass. '40.

Harvey, D.C. Colonization of Canada. 154p. Clarke, Irwin & Co. Toronto, Canada. '36.

Higham, John. Strangers in the land. Patterns of American nativism, 1860-1925. 431p. Rutgers University Press. New Brunswick, N.J. '55.

Hoehler, F. K. Europe's homeless millions. (Headline Series no54) 96p. Foreign Policy Association. 345 E. 46th St. New York 17. '45.

Humphrey, H. H. Jr. Stranger at our gate. (Public Affairs Pamphlet no202) 28p. Public Affairs Committee. 22 E. 38th St. New York 16. '54.

Indiana University. Bureau of Public Discussion. Immigration—how wide shall we open the door? (Package Library brief and study outline) 9p. mimeo. The Bureau. Bloomington, Ind. '54.

Indiana University. Bureau of Public Discussion. Plight of the refugee. (Package Library study outline) 6p. mimeo. The Bureau. Bloomington, Ind. '54.

International Institute for the Unification of Private Law (UNIDROIT). Systematic compilation of international instruments relating to the legal status of aliens, United States of America; prepared at request of the United Nations. 478p. The Institute. Rome. '54.

Isaacs, Julius. Economics of migration. 297p. Oxford University Press. Toronto, Canada. '47.

Jerome, Harry. Migration and business cycles. (Publication no9) 256p. National Bureau of Economic Research. 261 Madison Ave. New York 16. '26.

Kalnay, Francis and Collins, Richard. New American. 388p. Greenberg. New York. '41.

Konvitz, M. R. Civil rights in immigration. (Cornell studies in civil liberty) 216p. Cornell University Press. Ithaca, N.Y. '53.

Kohler, M. J. Immigration and aliens in the United States. 459p. Bloch Publishing Co. New York. '36.

Kuznets, Simon and Rubin, Ernest. Immigration and the foreign born. (Occasional Paper no46) 107p. National Bureau of Economic Research. 261 Madison Ave. New York 16. '54.

Landis, P. H. Population problems. 500p. American Book Company. New York. '43.

Laughlin, H. H. Immigration and conquest. 267p. Chamber of Commerce of the State of New York. New York. '39.

Lorimer, Frank; Winston, E. E. B. and Kiser, L. K. Foundations of American population policy. 178p. Harper & Bros. New York. '40.

Lorimer, Frank and Osborn, Frederick. Dynamics of population. 461p. Macmillan. New York. '34.

Lubell, Samuel. Future of American politics. 285p. Harper & Bros. New York. '52.

Maslow, Will, and Waldman, Lois. Analysis of the racist origins of the national quota system of the immigration act of 1924. 28p. American Jewish Congress. 15 E. 84th St. New York 28. '52.

Mayer-Daxlanden, Hans. Status of American citizenship and the future of immigration. 64p. Savoy Book Publishers. New York. '41.

McLellan, M. B. and De Bonis, A. V. Within our gates. 304p. Harper & Bros. New York. '40.

Mukerjee, Radhakamal. Political economy of population. 467p. Longmans, Green. London, England. '45.

Murphy, J. C. Analysis of the attitudes of the American Catholic toward the immigrant and the Negro. 1825-1925. 158p. Catholic University of America Press. Washington, D.C. '40.

Myrdal, Gunnar. Population, a problem for democracy. 237p. Harvard University Press. Cambridge, Mass. '40.

National Community Relations Advisory Council. New omnibus immigration and nationality bills in Senate and House. (NCRAC Bulletin no 18) 8p. The Council. 9 E. 38th St. New York 16. '53.

National Community Relations Advisory Council. Report of the President's commission on immigration and naturalization. (NCRAC Bulletin no 16) 6p. The Council. 9 E. 38th St. New York 16. '53.

National Economic Council. What about immigration? (Economic Council Letter no 171) 4p. The Council. 350 5th Ave. New York 1. '47.

National Economic Council. Stop these two bills! (Economic Council Letter no335) 4p. The Council. 350 5th Ave. New York 1. '54.

New York Society for Ethical Culture. Trespassers—or good neighbors? 8p. The Society. 2 W. 64th St. New York 23. '55.

Newweek Club and Educational Bureaus. Immigration: is the McCarran Act the answer? 23p. (Platform Study Guide) The Bureaus. 152 W. 42d St. New York 36. '53.

Perry, G. S. Families of America: where they came from and how they live. 151p. McGraw-Hill. New York. '49.

Peters, C. A. Immigration problem. (Reference shelf. v 19, no7) 254p. H. W. Wilson Co. New York. '48.

Saenger, Gerhart. Today's refugees, tomorrow's citizens. 286p. Harper & Bros. New York. '41.

Saveth, E. N. American historians and European immigrants, 1875-1925. 244p. Columbia University Press. New York. '48.

Saveth, E. N. Understanding the American past. 613p. Little, Brown & Co. Boston. '54.

Seabrook, W. B. These foreigners. 358p. Harcourt, Brace & Co. New York. '38.

*Seaver, C. H. As we do unto others. 32p. National Council of the Churches of Christ in the United States of America. 120 E. 23d St. New York 10. '52.

Sellin, Henry ed. Proceedings of the New York University conference on practice and procedure under the Immigration and Nationality Act (McCarran-Walter) held June 13, 1953, under auspices of the Division of General Education and the School of Law. 145p. Oceana Publications. Published for New York University Press. New York. '54.

Shippen, K. B. Passage to America: the story of the great migrations. 211p. Harper & Bros. New York. '50.

Simpson, J. H. Refugee problem. 637p. Oxford University Press. New York. '39.

Smith, W. C. Americans in the making: the natural history of the assimilation of immigrants. 454p. Appleton-Century. New York. '39.

Stegner, Wallace. One nation. 340p. Houghton Mifflin. Boston. '45.

Taft, D. R. Human migration. 590p. Ronald Press. New York. '36.

Thompson, W. S. Population problems. 471p. McGraw-Hill. New York. '42.

Toye, O. J. Measuring up. 77p. mimeo. Usher Publications. Boston. '53.

United Nations. Department of Social Affairs. Population Division. Elements of immigration policy. 21p. United Nations. New York. '54.

United States. Congress. Committee on the Judiciary. Comparative print of the texts of the Immigration and Nationality Act and immigration and nationality laws existing prior to enactment of public law 414. 252p. United States Government Printing Office. Washington 25, D.C. '52.

United States. Department of Justice. Immigration and Naturalization Service. Naturalization laws. 442p. United States Government Printing Office. Washington 25, D.C. '53.

United States. President's Commission on Immigration and Naturalization. Hearings, September 30-October 29, 1952, printed for the use of the Committee on the Judiciary. House of Representatives. 2v. 2089p. United States Government Printing Office. Washington 25, D.C. '52.

United States. President's Commission on Immigration and Naturalization. Whom we shall welcome; report of the Commission, including text of the President's veto. 319p. United States Government Printing Office. Washington 25, D.C. '52.

*Van Kirk, W. W. Immigration and Nationality Act of 1952. 8p. Community Relations Service. 386 4th Ave. New York 16. '54.

Wilcox, W. F. ed. International migrations. 2v. 1828p. National Bureau of Economic Research. 261 Madison Ave. New York 16. '29, '31.

Wittke, C. F. We who built America. 527p. Prentice-Hall. New York. '39.

Young, D. R. American minority people. 621p. Harper & Bros. New York. '32.

Ziegler, B. M. Immigration, an American dilemma. 118p. D. C. Heath & Co. Boston. '53.

PERIODICALS

America. 88:563. F. 21, '53. Catholic views on our immigration law. C. S. Mihanovich.

America. 90:587. Mr. 6, '54. And now *Braceros.*

America. 91:331. Je. 26, '54. Italian view of the United States immigration policy.

America. 91:495-7. Ag. 21, '54. Deporting our subversive aliens. R. F. Drinan.

America. 92:520. F. 12, '55. Roadblocks for refugees. V. J. Proeller.

America. 93:255. Je. 4, '55. Immigration and Christian morals.

American Journal of International Law. 48:193-221. Ap. '54. International protection of refugees. Paul Weis.

American Journal of International Law. 49:87-8. Ja. '55. Naturalization: effect of exemption from military service.

American Legion Magazine. 54:33. Mr. '53. About M'Carran-Walter Act. A. B. Willard.

*American Legion Magazine. 56:24-5+. My. '54. What is 100% Americanism? R. B. Pitkin.

American Magazine. 150:36-7+. O. '50. We are nursing a red fifth column. W. B. Miller.

American Mercury. 72:556-63. My. '51. Isle of detention. W. L. White.

American Mercury. 81:51-7. O. '55. Immigration, 1956 issue. J. B. Matthews.

*Annals of the American Academy of Political and Social Science. 262: 1-192. Mr. '49. Reappraising our immigration policy. Hugh Carter, ed.

> *Reprinted in this book:* Immigration policy prior to World War I. Carl Wittke. p5-14; International implications of American immigration policy. Paul Wiers. p39-44; Agencies organized by nationality groups in the United States. Y. J. Chyz and Read Lewis. p 148-58.

Atlantic Monthly. 191:27-31. My. '53. We need more immigrants. Oscar Handlin.

> *Discussion.* 192:19. Jl. '53.

Atlantic Monthly. 192:8. S. '53. Unlocking the door.

Bulletin of the Atomic Scientists. 8:no7. O. '52. American visa policy and foreign scientists. E. A. Shils, ed.

> Entire issue.

*Business Week. p 150-2. My. 2, '53. Puerto Ricans start up labor ladder.

Business Week. p62-4+. O. 24, '53. Wetbacks in middle of border war.

Christendom. 11:316-26. Jl. '46. Cultural pluralism in the American tradition. W. W. Sweet.

Christian Century. 70:275. Mr. 11, '53. McCarran Act revision a church priority.

> *Reply.* 70:419. Ap. 8, '53. P. McCarran.

Christian Century. 71:461-2. Ap. 14, '54. Congress bows to a church; bills for the relief of Roman Catholic nuns.

Christian Century. 71:1423-5. N. 27, '54. You stand at the gate to America.

Christian Century. 72:196. F. 16, '55. Is the Refugee Relief Act a deliberate fake?
   Reply. 72:336-7. Mr. 16, '55. S. McLeod.

Christian Century. 72:300-1. Mr. 9, '55. Stranger, when? Martin Schroeder.

Collier's. 118:24-6+. Ag. 17, '46. Rio Grande, river of death. Don Hinga.

Collier's. 131:70. F. 28, '53. If this be liberty . . .

Columbia Law Review. 53:451-75. Ap. '53. Loss of citizenship by continuous residence abroad. E. I. Gordon.

Columbia Law Review. 55:311-41. Mr. '55. American immigration policy. C. P. Schwartz.

Commentary. 3:1-6. Ja. '47. Democracy needs the open door; immigration and America's future. Oscar Handlin.

Commentary. 14:492-500. N. '52. Third generation in America. M. L. Hansen.

Commentary. 19:120-7. F. '53. How to remedy our Puerto Rican problem. Charles Abrams.

*Commentary. 15:401-8. Ap. '53. America's ethnic pattern; melting pot or nation of nations? Nathan Glazer.

Commentary. 20:77-86. Jl. '55. "Scientific" basis of our immigration policy. William Petersen.

Commentary. 20:101-8. Ag. '55. "Triple Melting Pot." Will Herberg.

Commonweal. 55:31-3. O. 19, '51. Right to emigrate. G. W. C. Ross.

Commonweal. 57:345. Ja. 9, '53. New basis for immigration; abolition of national quotas.

Commonweal. 59:9-11. O. 9, '53. Puerto Ricans come to Youngstown. J. E. Koch.

Commonweal. 59:571-4. Mr. 12, '54. Unwelcome aliens. H. M. Siegel.

Commonweal. 60:598. S. 24, '54. These inaccessible shores: Refugee Relief Act and McCarran-Walter Act.

Congress Weekly. 20:5-8. Ja. 12, '53. For a new immigration policy, the commission points the way. Phil Baum.

Congressional Quarterly. 13:347-54. Ap. 8, '55. Immigration.

Contemporary Review. 167:112-18. F. '45. Economic value of refugees. Israel Cohen.

Cornell Law Quarterly. 39:517-25. Spring '54. Immigration: nationality: good moral character: effect of traffic violations.

Cornell Law Quarterly. 40:365-9. Winter '55. Constitutional law: expatriation and dual citizenship.

Coronet. 28:164+. Je. '50. Immigrant's credo; faith in America. Eugene Davis.

Economic Outlook. 13:73-80. N. '52. McCarran immigration law violates American traditions.

Federal Rules Decisions. 14:105-40. Je. '53. Immigration and nationality systems of the United States of America. H. B. Hazard.

Fordham Law Review. 23:243-95. D. '54. Dual nationality: with particular reference to the citizenship status of the Italo-American.

Foreign Policy Reports. 23:14-20. Ap. 1, '47. Immigration policy of the United States. E. G. Harrison.

Foreign Policy Reports. 23:20. Ap. 1, '47. Race limitations in immigration and naturalization laws. Charles Gordon.

*Foreign Policy Reports. 26:190-9. Ja. 15, '51. World's refugee problem. F. W. Riggs.

Foreign Policy Reports. 26:200. Ja. 15, '51. U. S. displaced persons program. F. W. Riggs.

Foreign Service Journal. p28-30. O. '53. Visa work under the displaced persons act. M. E. Blake, Jr.

Free World. 9:31-3. F. '45. Immigration and future security. Norman Angell.

Gavel [Milwaukee Bar Association]. 14:6-11. Ap. '53. Immigration and Nationality Act of 1952: critical analysis. W. C. Dill.

George Washington Law Review. 22:217-41. D. '53. Immigration and Nationality Act of 1952 and the alien crewman.

Georgia Law Journal. 41:63-90. N. '52. Passports and freedom of travel: the conflict of a right and a privilege.

Georgia Law Journal. 41:364-93. Mr. '53. Our immigration laws: a continuing affront to the administrative procedure act.

Harper's Magazine. 201:39-46. Jl. '50. Perpetual refugees. M. L. Hoffman.

Harper's Magazine. 206:78-83. My. '53. New York and the Puerto Ricans; with editorial comment. Winifred Raushenbush.

Harper's Magazine. 210:27-32. Mr. '55. America's next twenty years: coming labor shortage. P. F. Drucker.
    Discussion. 210:4+. My. '55.

*Harper's Magazine. 210:68-72. Ap. '55. That phony refugee law. Cabell Phillips.

*I & N Reporter [Immigration and Naturalization Reporter]. 4:6-9. Jl. '55. Immigration today. F. L. Auerbach.

*Information Service. 32:2-3. Ap. 4, '53. "Give me your tired, your poor—".

International Labor Review. 59:367-93. Ap. '49. The ILO manpower programme.

International Labor Review. 62:91-115. Ag. '50. Migration and economic development.

Interpreter Releases. 23:280-4. N. 12, '46. Problem of Europe's displaced persons. E. G. Harrison.

Interpreter Releases. 30:225-40. Ag. 5, '53. Refugee Relief Act of 1953.

Interpreter Releases. 31:16-25. Ja. 19, '54. Aliens and foreign born. F. L. Auerbach.

Interpreter Releases. 32:1-7. Ja. 7, '55. Immigration: the alien and the bill of rights. E. J. Ennis.

Interpreter Releases. 32:250-6. Jl. 7, '55. Denial of passport held subject to judicial review.

Jewish Frontier. 20:21-6. O. '53. Refugee Relief Act of 1953. Sidney Liskofsky.

Jewish Social Service Quarterly. 30:421-6. Summer '54. Public Law 414—the McCarran-Walter Act—or the Immigration and Nationality Act of 1952. A. S. Petluck.

Journal of the Bar Association of the District of Columbia. 20:325-33. Jl.-Ag. '53. Immigration and nationality act of 1952. David Carliner.

Judge Advocate General's Journal. p 14-20. D. '54. McCarran act: aspects of immigration and nationality of interest to the serviceman. L. B. Watson.

Lawyer's Guild Review. 13:79-83. Spring '53. McCarran-Walter Act. J. W. Porter.

Life. 30:33-7. My. 21, '51. Wetbacks swarm in.

Life. 36:26-9. F. 15, '54. Bulge of *Braceros* at the border.

Life. 38:45. Ap. 25, '55. Immigration, the real issue is an evil law.

Look. 17:75-9. N. 17, '53. Aliens are swarming over our unguarded northern border. A. G. Maisel.

Look. 19:22-5. F. 8, '55. Our iron curtain is turning friends into enemies.

Michigan Law Review. 51:881-902. Ap. '53. Constitutional law: denaturalization under the Immigration and Nationality Act of 1952.

Milbank Memorial Fund Quarterly. 25:174-88. Ap. '47. Demographic and economic implications of larger immigration. W. S. Thompson.

Minnesota Law Review. 37:440-58. My. '53. Constitutional restraints on the expulsion and exclusion of aliens.

*Monetary Times [Toronto, Canada]. 122:22-6+. S. '54. 30,000,000 people in Canada by 1975? Carleton Ketchum.

Monthly Labor Review. 76:45-7. Ja. '53. Recommendations on immigration policy.

Montreal Star Weekend Magazine. p2+. S. 11, '54. Our million immigrants are changing Canada. Robert McKeown.

Montreal Star Weekend Magazine. p23+. S. 18, '54. They hustle and it pays off. Robert McKeown.

Montreal Star Weekend Magazine. p 11+. S. 25, '54. Canadians or aliens? Robert McKeown.

Nation. 174:299-301. Mr. 29, '52. McCarran's iron curtain; Walter-McCarran bills. Alex Brooks.

Nation. 179:462-3. N. 27, '54. Consular curtain; visa policy. J. C. Bruce.

Nation. 180:258-64. Mr. 26, '55. Deportation deliriums. L. B. Frantz.

Nation. 180:inside cover. Ap. 9, '55. Ferment in the lettuce fields, Imperial valley. William Carpenter.

National Lawyer's Guild Quarterly. 2:171-92. Spring '39. Social and economic consequences of exclusionary immigration laws. F. S. Cohen.

National Republic. 40:17-18+. D. '52. Plot against the McCarran-Walter Act. H. G. Moore.

National Republic. 40:23-4. F. '53. Walter blasts commission report.

National Republic. 41:1-2+. N. '53. Help us save the McCarran-Walter Act. Herman Welker.

Nation's Business. 43:88-91. Ag. '55. Freedom's new danger: too many people.

New Republic. 128:8-9. F. 16, '53. National origin; fraud and threat. H. H. Lehman.

New Republic. 130:3-4. F. 22, '54. Chicago's Puerto Ricans.

New Republic. 131:16-18. Ag. 23, '54. Puerto Rico in Harlem. Geoffrey Wagner.

New Republic. 132:3. Ap. 20, '55. Orphans, Greeks, Republicans and McLeod.

New Republic. 133:5-6. S. 19, '55. U. S. counterpart to the iron curtain.

Newsweek. 41:56. My. 25, '53. Wetback flood.

Newsweek. 42:26. Ag. 31, '53. New wetback answers?

Newsweek. 43:22+. Je. 28, '54. War with the wetbacks.

*New York Herald Tribune. p3, S. 29; p3, S. 30, '53. Stream of aliens pours into the United States from Canada. J. G. Rogers.

*New York Journal-American. p 19. Jl. 27, '55. Changes would imperil security. F. E. Walter.

*New York Journal-American. p 18. Jl. 28, '55. Refugee program a dreary failure. H. H. Lehman.

New York Times. p 13. Ap. 26, '55. United States defeat seen in exiles' misery.

*New York Times. p 1+. Je. 10, '55. Lawyer named to refugee post with orders to speed entries. W. H. Lawrence.

New York Times. pE8. Ag. 28, '55. Bad immigration law.

New York Times Magazine. p8+. Jl. 8, '51. Let us open again the gates. J. K. Javits.

New York Times Magazine. p 12-13+. My. 24, '53. Visa to America; a McCarran act drama.

*New York Times Magazine. p 13+. Ja. 31, '54. Two every minute across the border. Gladwin Hill.

Reader's Digest. 59:91-4. Ag. '51. Why shouldn't they be Americans? Blake Clark.

Reader's Digest. 59:147-68. S. '51. Penny from heaven. Max Winkler. *Abridged.*

*Reader's Digest. 62:61-5. F. '53. Puerto Rican problem in New York. Blake Clark.

*Reader's Digest. 62:126-32. My. '53. Truth about the immigration act. F. E. Walter.

Reader's Digest. 64:1-7. Ja. '54. Our shabby welcome to foreigners. Lester Velie.

Reader's Digest. 64:11-14. F. '54. *Caramba.* I'm a lucky guy! Michael Scully.

*Reader's Digest. 65:61-6. Ag. '54. America's new front-door policy. H. J. L'Heureux.

Reporter. 8:3. Ja. 20, '53. On subversion.

Reporter. 10:26-8. Ja. 19, '54. Lower depths of upper Broadway. Anzia Yezierska.

*Reporter. 10:28-32. Ap. 13, '54. Hungry workers, ripe crops, and the nonexistent Mexican border. R. P. Eckels.

Reporter. 12:10-17. My. 5, '55. My ninety days in Washington. Edward Corsi.
    Discussion. 12:5. Je. 2, '55.

Reporter. 12:22-6. Je. 2, '55. Let's talk about immigration. Edward Corsi.

Reporter. 13:23-7. S. 22, '55. How Canada welcomes immigrants. Robert Crichton.

Rotarian. 84:12-13+. Je. '54. Should the United Nations control immigration? L. D. Luckmann and J. R. Tiffany.

Rotarian. 85:14-15. D. '54. Background of a citizen. C. B. Kelland.

St. John's Law Review. 28:63-73. D. '53. Some problems of dual nationality.

Saturday Evening Post. 224:16-17+. D. 22, '51. Uncle Sam's bouncers get tough. Richard English.

Saturday Evening Post. 225:10. F. 21, '53. Before attacking immigration law, why not read it?

Saturday Evening Post. 224:22-3+. Ja. 12, '54. Texas tackles the race problem. T. S. Sutherland.

Saturday Evening Post. 226:12. Je. 19, '54. McCarran Act will bar no genuine visiting scientists.
    Reply. Science. 120:465-6. S. 17, '54. Scientists and the McCarran Act. Otto Struve.

Saturday Evening Post. 227:42-3+. Je. 11, '55. Reds want them back! C. W. Thayer.

Scholastic. 62:10-12. F. 4, '53. Whom shall we welcome?

Science. 117:287-9. Mr. 20, '53. New immigration law. W. A. W. Krebs, Jr. and C. P. Ebb.

Science. 120:465-6. S. 17, '54. Scientists and the McCarran Act. Otto Struve.

Shingle [Philadelphia Bar Association]. 16:274-7. D. '53. Trends in immigration and nationality legislation. F. B. Masino.

Social Order. 3:405-6. N. '53. Proposed new immigration law. C. S. Mihanovich.

Social Research. 14:45-58. Mr. '47. Displaced persons; a human tragedy of World War II. J. A. Berger.

Stanford Law Review. 6:287-322. Mr. '54. Wetbacks: can the states act to curb illegal entry?

Survey. 87:463-5. N. '51. Call for a new immigration policy. Chester Bowles.

Taxes. 31:795-817. O. '53. Aliens and the U. S. income tax law. H. Schneider.

Temple Law Quarterly. 27:62-89. Summer '53. Immigration and Nationality Act of 1952: our new alien and sedition law. Joseph Wasserman.

This Week. p7+. Ja. 31, '54. Uncle Sam rushes the bums. Richard English.

Time. 61:29. Ap. 27, '53. Ants; Mexican wetbacks.

Time. 62:19. Jl. 13, '53. Pat and Herman: emergency migration bill.

Time. 62:10. Ag. 3, '53. Message from the cloakroom; Pat McCarran and Arthur Watkins compromise.

Time. 64:19. Jl. 19, '54. So heinous, so infamous.

*Time. 65:19. Ap. 25, '55. 90-Day wonder.

Time. 65:36. My. 2, '55. Coyote's bite.

Today's Health. 31:30-4. F. '52. Spanish Harlem. A. V. Jahr.

U. S. A.—The Magazine of American Affairs. 2:32-40. F. '53. Background of the McCarran-Walter Act. Pat McCarran.

United Nations World. 1:4-5. Je. '47. Refugees: the solution as F. D. R. saw it. Ladislas Farago.

*United States Department of State Bulletin. 27:78-82. Jl. 14, '52. Immigration and nationality act vetoed. H. S. Truman.

United States Department of State Bulletin. 27:195-239. F. 2, '53. Visa work of the department of state and the foreign service. E. B. Coulter.

United States Department of State Bulletin. 28:642-6. My. 4, '53. Visa function under the immigration and nationality bill. F. L. Auerbach.

United States Department of State Bulletin. 28:857-9. Je. 15, '53. President's proposal for admission of European migrants. W. B. Smith.

United States Department of State Bulletin. 30:467-8. Mr. 29, '54. U.S.-Mexican agreement on farm labor; joint statement, with statement by President Eisenhower.

*United States Department of State Bulletin. 30:599-602. Ap. 19, '54. New trends in American immigration. E. S. Maney.

United States Department of State Bulletin. 32:415-19. Mr. 14, '55. Assistance to escapees—its significance for America. D. D. Houghton.

United States Department of State Bulletin. 32:701. Ap. 25, '55. United States-Mexican agreement on migratory workers.

United States Department of State Bulletin. 32:951-3. Je. 13, '55. Recommendations for amending Refugee Relief Act; message to Congress on May 27, 1955. D. D. Eisenhower.

United States Department of State Bulletin. 32:1047-50. Je. 27, '55. Immigration today. F. L. Auerbach.

United States News & World Report. 33:26. O. 31, '52. Why immigration is in politics.

United States News & World Report. 38:46-7. Ap. 29, '55. Who's getting into the United States now?

University of Pittsburgh Law Review. 14:428-37. Spring '53. Deportation under the Immigration and Nationality Act of 1952.

Utah Law Review. 3:349-57. Spring '53. Rights of aliens in exclusion proceedings.

Virginia Law Review. 40:853-73. N. '54. Right to go abroad: to have and to hold a passport.

Vital Speeches of the Day. 13:607-8. Jl. 15, '47. Admission of displaced persons. Message to Congress July 7, '47. H. S. Truman.

World Frontiers. 2:22-8. Summer '53. McCarran-Walter act. Winifred Armstrong.

Yale Law Journal. 59:139. D. '49. Section 404 (c) of the nationality act of 1940: residence abroad as automatic expatriation of the naturalized American.

Yale Law Journal. 62:845-52. Ap. '53. Protecting deportable aliens from physical persecution: section 243 (h) of the Immigration and Nationality Act of 1952.

DATE DUE